AT HOME

AT HOME

My favourite recipes for family & friends

MONICA GALETTI

aster

For all my family and friends, near and far.

First published in Great Britain in 2021 by Aster, an imprint of
Octopus Publishing Group Ltd
Carmelite House, 50 Victoria Embankment
London EC4Y 0DZ
www.octopusbooks.co.uk

An Hachette UK Company www.hachette.co.uk

ISBN 978 1 78325 487 3

A CIP catalogue record for this book is available from the British Library.

Printed and bound in Italy
10 9 8 7 6 5 4 3 2 1

Publisher: Stephanie Jackson
Senior Managing Editor: Sybella Stephens
Copy Editor: Jo Richardson
Art Director: Juliette Norsworthy
Photographer: Yuki Sugiura
Food Stylist: Monica Galetti
Home Economist: Karen Taylor
Props Stylist: Jennifer Haslam
Hair & Make-up: Topaz Knight
Senior Production Manager: Peter Hunt

COOK'S NOTES

In some recipes both whole eggs and measurements are given for eggs. Egg yolks
and whites can vary in size, so I often weigh my eggs for accuracy. Approximate
conversions are as follows: 1 medium egg yolk = 20g, 1 medium egg white = 30g.

All recipes have been tested using a fan-assisted oven and Gas Mark temperatures
are equivalent to these. For conventional ovens, if you do not have a fan function,
increase the temperature by 20 degrees or check the manufacturer's handbook,
although the same results cannot be guaranteed.

CONTENTS

INTRODUCTION

My life as a chef, restaurateur and occasional television presenter makes for a pretty organized but crazy schedule. I love it, and although at times it's difficult to balance it has been very rewarding and educational on both a professional and personal level. When I am at home, I like to really let go of the stresses and enjoy a little bit of the simple life with my family and friends, cooking and laughing together.

My love of food began in Samoa where I was born. To this day I recall the tropical smells from the fruits and plantation to the Sunday feasts we would eat, called *toana'i*. Fortunately, when we moved to New Zealand, our Samoan culture thrived and we still managed to enjoy a few of our traditional dishes. However, adjusting to the different tastes and smells of the food there took a little getting used to. It was in New Zealand where I recall cousins coming to stay and my Mum knocking up a batch of her cookies for us all. My Dad still loved to grow his own fruit and vegetables, so I've grown up used to regularly eating fresh vegetables – something you appreciate so much more when you get older (thanks, Dad)! Meal times were always together around the table, and it's something I love to do to this day with my own family. Eating and catching up on the day's events is such a wonderful way to end the day, helped by a nice glass of wine now and then.

In our household, we are very easy going about what we have for meals. Weekends are our favourite time, as we're usually all together on Sundays. We almost always have a plan for what we're going to eat. My daughter Anais may decide to make a dessert and David, my husband (who is now a very good cook) might decide to cure a side of salmon. Sunday is also normally bread day, when the sourdough for the week is baked first thing – I love the aromas of Sunday mornings in our house!

During the week I think we are like any other household, busy with school, work and life in general. This is why we like quick-fix dinners, so we can enjoy the precious time we have together, instead of spending hours in the kitchen. So, to keep things running smoothly, we try and shop for the week ahead – salmon, chicken thighs, maybe some steak and plenty of fruit and veg, so we can open the fridge and say, right... let's do this! We always have eggs and pasta ready for when we are not that hungry or maybe if we just fancy an omelette.

We also love spending time with our close friends who are like family to us. Oddly, they like spending time with us, plus they love food and wine in equal measures! Enjoying great food in great company will always be at the top of my list of favourite things to do when I'm not working.

So, with all this in mind, it was time to share with you what has resulted in this book

– me at home. It was really fun working on it because, as I was selecting the recipes, they would remind me of a certain memory or people I had shared that meal with: a real trip down memory lane for me and I'd remember a funny story or conversation that took place.

I hope you will find one or two of these recipes not only enjoyable, but that they will create some happy memories for you when you make them.

And do as we say in Samoan, after we say grace at meal time: *ai loa* – eat now!

Breakfast in our household throughout the week is not normally a chilled time. Well, actually it mostly is for my daughter Anais, but my husband David and I are always on the go, and so when we do get mornings together at home free from work, this is our chilled time. And we love it! I think we only truly appreciate these times when we rarely get them. Which can also be said for how we feel about many other things in life.

Both David and I come from families who enjoy time around the table, talking and planning the rest of the day or week. So being able to do this with Anais, when we both work such crazy hours, is a very important part of how we come together as a family.

During the working week we eat much lighter, quicker breakfasts, such as the Samoan shortbread from the pantry with yogurt. A smoothie is a nice fast option too, but in this chapter I've also included some of the more indulgent favourites we treat ourselves to every now and then.

CHILLED-OUT BREAKFASTS

CONTENTS

Did someone say waffles?! This is the usual remark from my daughter when we knock up a batch of these, normally when I see a few bananas left in the fruit bowl starting to overripen and no one seems to want to eat them. When my husband makes them, he ALWAYS doubles the recipe and we end up with far more than we need, so I tend to put the leftovers in the freezer to reheat in the toaster on weekdays. For toppings, we mix it up with anything from bacon and golden syrup to berries or homemade Chocolate Hazelnut Spread (see page 17).

BANANA WAFFLES

MAKES 20

180g plain flour

12g baking powder

30g caster sugar

pinch of ground cinnamon

pinch of ground nutmeg

pinch of salt

230ml milk

seeds scraped from 1 vanilla pod

3 eggs, separated

50g unsalted butter, melted

3 ripe bananas, mashed to a thick purée

rapeseed oil

1 Mix all the dry ingredients together in a large bowl and make a well in the centre.

2 Whisk in the milk, vanilla seeds, egg yolks and melted butter to combine, then stir in the mashed bananas.

3 In a separate bowl, whisk the egg whites to stiff peaks using an electric hand whisk, then fold into the batter.

4 Preheat your waffle maker and wipe with a little oil.

5 Pour the batter into the waffle maker, seal and cook until golden (about 5 minutes, or according to the manufacturer's instructions). Repeat with the remaining batter, oiling the waffle maker between batches. Serve the waffles warm with your favourite toppings.

Oh my, these have got to be one of my favourite Samoan doughnuts. In Samoan, we call them *pani keke* – which, when you say it aloud, sounds like 'pancakes'. My Auntie Nive used to make batches of them when I was a kid, and even now when I visit New Zealand you'll find me at the front of the queue at her market stall waiting to buy them. She always gives me a few extra and I've finally given up on insisting on paying for them. Here at home, I have to make them myself, of course.

COCONUT DOUGHNUTS

MAKES 8 LARGE DOUGHNUTS

8g fresh yeast, crumbled, or fast-action dried yeast

215g strong white flour

40g caster sugar

pinch of salt

50ml coconut milk

2 medium egg yolks (40g in total)

40ml warm water

rapeseed oil, for deep-frying

FOR THE COCONUT FILLING

90g caster sugar

25g soft unsalted butter

150ml coconut cream

50g desiccated coconut, toasted

FOR THE CINNAMON SUGAR

50g caster sugar

1 teaspoon ground cinnamon

1   Place the yeast, flour, sugar and salt in a bowl. Add the coconut milk and egg yolks and beat to a smooth dough. Add the warm water slowly while mixing, until combined. Cover and leave in a warm place for 45 minutes–1 hour or until doubled in size.

2   Meanwhile, make the coconut filling. Place the sugar in a heavy-based saucepan and cook over a medium heat to a caramel, then whisk in the butter. Whisk continuously to a thick bubbling sauce, then add the coconut cream gradually, whisking after each addition. Stir in the desiccated coconut, then set aside to cool.

3   Divide the dough into 8 and roll into small balls. Place on a tray, cover and leave in a warm place for about 30 minutes or until doubled in size.

4   Heat the oil in a deep saucepan to 165°C (make sure the pan is no more than one-third full with oil). Deep-fry the doughnuts 2 at a time for 4–5 minutes, turning now and then, until golden brown. Drain on kitchen paper.

5   Place a long-tipped piping nozzle in the base of a piping bag and fill the bag with the coconut filling. Pipe a little of the coconut filling into the centre of each doughnut.

6   For the cinnamon sugar, mix the sugar and cinnamon together. Toss the doughnuts in the cinnamon sugar while still warm, then shake off the excess before serving.

This is a simple family favourite of ours, usually reserved for Sundays but also enjoyed on many family mornings together. My secret ingredient is the addition of Cointreau! I make the crêpe batter by eye, but my husband likes to weigh everything out. The secret to a good crêpe batter is not to make the mixture too thick, so it covers the pan base in a thin coating. The chocolate hazelnut spread can be made using other nuts, or milk chocolate instead of dark, and in bigger batches so that there is plenty left over. You can reserve some of the toasted hazelnuts and then grate them over the top of a crêpe stack smothered in the spread.

CRÊPES WITH CHOCOLATE HAZELNUT SPREAD

MAKES 10 LARGE CRÊPES

375g plain flour

3 tablespoons caster sugar

600ml milk of your choice

3 eggs

60ml Cointreau or rum

rapeseed oil

FOR THE CHOCOLATE HAZELNUT SPREAD (MAKES 400G)

200g blanched hazelnuts

3 tablespoons olive oil

100g dark chocolate (70% cocoa), melted

2 tablespoons maple syrup or honey

1 teaspoon cocoa powder

seeds scraped from 1 vanilla pod

1   To make the chocolate hazelnut spread, preheat the oven to 180°C fan, Gas Mark 6.

2   Spread the hazelnuts out on a baking tray and roast for about 10 minutes, stirring halfway through.

3   Place the roasted nuts in a blender while still warm, add the olive oil and blend to a butter.

4   Add the remaining spread ingredients and continue blending until well combined. This can now be stored in a sterilized airtight jar for up to 7 days. (To sterilize jars, wash jars and lids in hot soapy water, preheat the oven to 140°C fan, Gas Mark 3, place the jars upside down on a baking tray and put it in the oven for 20 minutes. Meanwhile, boil a kettle and submerge the lids in boiling water in a bowl.)

5   Mix the flour and sugar together in a bowl and make a well in the centre. Pour in the milk while whisking.

6   Whisk in the eggs and Cointreau.

7   Preheat your crêpe pan over a medium heat. Add a little rapeseed oil, then wipe the pan with kitchen paper (this helps to create an even layer of oil and remove any excess).

8   Pour in the batter to make a thin coating and cook for about 30 seconds or until the underside is golden. Flip and cook for about 30 seconds on the other side, then set the crêpe aside. Repeat until all the batter is used up, oiling the pan again as needed. Serve the crêpes warm with the chocolate hazelnut spread.

Homemade granola is great, as I know exactly what's in it and there's no worry about any hidden sweeteners. Manuka honey is one of my favourite ingredients from New Zealand, but you can add whatever honey you want here. Use the recipe as a guide, adapting and changing the quantities according to your own preference – the most important thing is that you're happy with the mix of dried fruits and nuts. Serve with yogurt, or on top of the Smoothie Overnight Oats (see page 22) with fresh fruit.

MANUKA SPICED GRANOLA

SERVES 8–10

100g coconut oil

2 tablespoons manuka honey

1½ teaspoons ras el hanout

250g rolled oats

150g ready-to-eat dried apricots, chopped

125g walnuts, chopped

125g almonds, chopped

125g coconut flakes

100g sunflower seeds

2 tablespoons flaxseeds

1   Preheat the oven to 180°C fan, Gas Mark 6.

2   Melt the coconut oil and honey with the ras el hanout in a saucepan over a low heat.

3   Mix all the remaining ingredients in a large bowl. Pour over the coconut oil and honey mixture and stir to coat. Pour on to a large baking tray and spread out.

4   Bake for 20 minutes, stirring occasionally.

5   Leave to cool on the tray, then break the granola up if it has stuck together. Store in an airtight container.

This dish reminds me of my dad. Always one for a bargain, he'd buy a bumper box of bananas and of course we could never get through them all, so they would become very ripe (which is how he loves them – black, speckled and sweet). I can just picture those boxes of bananas now... But I believe the main reason he bought them in bulk was so that he could always have a pot of this banana soup on the stove. So much so that for a few years I simply couldn't face eating it any more! These days, I see it not only as a great way to use up overripe bananas, but also as a fantastic addition stirred through porridge or natural yogurt, though I'm not sure my dad would agree. If you can't find sago or tapioca pearls in your local shop, order them online.

SUA FA'I – SAMOAN BANANA SOUP

SERVES 4

3 ripe bananas, mashed

100g sago or tapioca pearls

300ml water

150ml coconut milk

½ lemon, for squeezing

honey or demerara sugar (optional)

1 Place the mashed bananas in a saucepan with the pearls and pour in the water.

2 Bring to the boil, then reduce the heat to a gentle simmer, stirring now and then. Cook for 20 minutes over a low heat or until the pearls become transparent, stirring often.

3 Stir in the coconut milk and season with a few drops of lemon juice. Add some honey or demerara sugar if you prefer it sweeter. Serve warm or cold.

I find this a great way to use up excess smoothie (not uncommon at our house – my daughter always makes too much!). These overnight oats are perfect for the morning rush: just pop a portion into a takeaway container and they'll set you up for the day. I like to add fresh fruit to the oats just before serving. Try blueberries (I love blueberries on everything), bananas or whatever you find in the fruit bowl.

SMOOTHIE OVERNIGHT OATS

SERVES 4–6

200g rolled oats

1 Granny Smith apple, grated

handful of sunflower seeds

2 tablespoons dried cranberries or any dried fruit

2 tablespoons chopped nuts

400ml leftover smoothie (see pages 23–4 or any other you may have)

100ml apple juice

1   Mix everything together, cover, then place in the refrigerator overnight.

Chocolate and bananas for breakfast? Works for me. And you can't beat a smoothie if you're on the go. When it's only breakfast time but it's already a busy day, this is an easy one to blitz and take away. (Option two: sometimes I ask my daughter to make one for me!) I use a lot of almond milk at home these days, as I'm a bit sensitive to dairy milk, so if you're like me it's a great alternative to have on hand. Soya milk is an excellent substitute if you prefer.

ALMOND MILK CHOCOLATE SMOOTHIE

SERVES 4–6

3 ripe bananas, chopped

170g rolled oats

400ml almond milk

2 teaspoons cocoa powder, plus extra to serve

ground nutmeg, to serve

1 Place all the ingredients except the nutmeg in a blender and blitz until smooth.

2 Dust with a little nutmeg and extra cocoa powder to serve.

In New Zealand spirulina is commonly used in cafés, so from a nostalgic point of view it's an ingredient I quite like to add to my smoothies – and of course it comes with significant health benefits (spirulina is considered a superfood thanks to its rich nutritional profile). This smoothie recipe is great for using up pretty much any ripe fruit if you don't have mangoes to hand – my daughter loves it with banana and blueberries.

MANGO SPIRULINA SMOOTHIE

SERVES 4

3 large ripe mangoes
400g Greek yogurt
350ml coconut milk
¼ teaspoon ground cardamom
1 tablespoon honey
1 teaspoon spirulina
juice of ½ lime

1 Slice the mangoes either side of their flat stones and discard the stones, then scoop the flesh into a blender.

2 Add all the remaining ingredients and blitz until smooth. Serve immediately.

Left: Mango Spirulina Smoothie;
Right: Almond Milk Chocolate Smoothie.

As a child, 'eggy bread' or French toast was one of my favourite things that my Mum used to make at weekends. As a treat we would have it with streaky bacon – delicious! Nowadays I use leftover homemade sourdough, since we don't actually buy bread very often, but as a throwback to the good old days, shop-bought sliced bread is fine to use here.

EGGY BREAD

SERVES 4

8 streaky bacon rashers

3 large eggs

200ml milk

2 pinches of salt

2 tablespoons chopped chives

8 bread slices

150g unsalted butter

1   Preheat the oven to 200°C fan, Gas Mark 7.

2   Place the bacon on a baking tray and cook for about 10 minutes or until crisp.

3   Meanwhile, whisk the eggs, milk, salt and chives together in a shallow bowl.

4   Preheat a nonstick frying pan over a medium heat.

5   Place 2 bread slices in the egg mixture to soak all over.

6   Add a knob of the butter to the pan and swirl to coat the base, then cook the egg-coated bread until golden on both sides. Repeat with the remaining bread, egg mixture and butter.

7   Serve topped with the crispy bacon.

These are made with a simple yeast bread dough. Funnily enough, I grew up knowing them as 'fried bread' and only later on realized they were called English muffins. If you love baking breads like I do, it's always preferable to make your own muffins for the Eggs Benedict (see page 28), but you can use shop-bought muffins if you're tight on time – it will still be delicious.

ENGLISH MUFFINS

MAKES 12

150ml milk

6g fresh yeast

30g caster sugar

250g plain flour, plus extra for dusting

rapeseed oil

1   Warm the milk in a saucepan. Crumble in the yeast, add the sugar and whisk until dissolved.

2   Place the flour in a bowl and make a well in the centre.

3   Pour the yeast mixture into the flour and gradually mix in to form a dough. Cover and leave in a warm place for an hour or until doubled in size.

4   Lightly flour your work surface and roll out the dough to about 5mm thick. Using a 7cm cutter, cut the dough into circles. Place on a large tray, cover and leave in a warm place for about an hour or until doubled in size.

5   Preheat the oven to 180°C fan, Gas Mark 6.

6   Lightly oil a nonstick frying pan and heat over a medium-high heat.

7   Fry the muffins for a few minutes on each side until golden brown. Transfer to a baking tray and bake for 3–4 minutes or until cooked through. Cool on a wire rack before serving.

As a young chef in my early twenties, we would finish work and all go out together, then end up in someone's kitchen knocking up eggs Benedict for a hangover cure. These days I'm not going out as much as I did back then, but I still love a fabulous eggs Benedict for breakfast. In New Zealand, a version of this can be found in practically every café you come across. And if you haven't tried sriracha before, a warning: it's addictive. We always keep a bottle in the house.

EGGS BENEDICT WITH SRIRACHA HOLLANDAISE

SERVES 4

1.5 litres water

75ml white wine vinegar

8 large eggs

4 English muffins (see page 27 for homemade), split

4–8 Serrano ham slices or similar

pepper

FOR THE HOLLANDAISE

100ml white wine vinegar

50ml water

1 tarragon sprig, chopped

1 tablespoon white peppercorns, crushed

250g butter

1 tablespoon hot sriracha

3 large egg yolks

½ lemon, for squeezing

salt

1　For the hollandaise, place the vinegar, water, tarragon and crushed peppercorns in a saucepan and reduce to one-third over a medium heat, then leave to cool.

2　Meanwhile, place the butter in a saucepan over a medium-low heat. Swirl to melt and wait until the yellow liquid has separated from the white dairy solids. Leave to cool slightly, then pour the yellow clarified butter into a jug, discarding the white solids.

3　Pour the vinegar mixture into a heatproof bowl and whisk in the sriracha and egg yolks. Place the bowl over a pan of gently simmering water and whisk for 5–8 minutes until very thick.

4　Take off the heat and whisk in the warm clarified butter. Season with a squeeze of lemon juice and a little salt. Keep warm over the pan of water off the heat, stirring occasionally, while you poach the eggs.

5　Place the 1.5 litres of water in a deep saucepan with the vinegar and bring to a simmer.

6　Crack the eggs into separate cups.

7　Swirl the simmering water to create a vortex – this helps form the egg into a nice round shape. Drop 1 or 2 eggs into the vortex and cook for 2–3 minutes. Remove with a slotted spoon. Repeat to cook the remaining eggs.

8　While the eggs are poaching, toast the muffin halves. Spread a little of the hollandaise on to the toasted muffins. Divide the ham and place on top, then add the poached eggs.

9　Cover generously with more hollandaise and finish with a twist of black pepper.

This is another childhood favourite of mine, and now one of my daughter's. We like pikelets served with either butter and jam, or fresh berries, whipped cream and a little manuka honey. When I was a kid, my dad would make these at weekends, as thick as possible (the thicker the pikelets, the fewer he'd have to make!), and serve them up hot and sweet, topped with butter – lots of it – and doused in golden syrup. This recipe works well with wholemeal self-raising flour, too.

PIKELETS

MAKES 10 LARGE OR 16 SMALL PIKELETS

250g self-raising flour

1½ teaspoons baking powder

50g caster sugar

pinch of salt

250ml milk

2 large eggs

rapeseed oil

1 Mix the dry ingredients together in a large bowl and make a well in the centre.

2 Pour in the milk and eggs while whisking until you have a smooth batter.

3 Preheat a large nonstick frying pan over a medium heat. Add a little oil and then wipe the pan with kitchen paper.

4 Using a spoon, drop rounds of batter from the point of a spoon on to the hot pan.

5 Cook over a medium heat until bubbles start to appear, then turn the pikelets over and cook until golden. Serve warm.

According to my daughter, these are the best! A pet hate of mine is overcooked dry scrambled eggs. One of the first things I taught my daughter Anais to make was perfect scrambled eggs – something so simple yet so easy to get wrong. Once you have perfected your scrambled eggs, there are lots of options to enjoy it with, one of my favourites being smoked salmon.

THE BEST SCRAMBLED EGGS!

SERVES 4

4 large sourdough bread slices

1 garlic clove, peeled

olive oil

12 large eggs

60ml double cream (optional)

40g unsalted butter

salt and pepper

chopped chives, to serve

1   Preheat a griddle pan over a medium-high heat.

2   Rub the sourdough slices all over with the garlic clove and drizzle both sides liberally with olive oil. Char them on the hot griddle pan on both sides, then set aside.

3   Heat a wide nonstick pan over a medium heat.

4   Break the eggs into a bowl, add the cream, if using, and lightly beat with a fork. Season with salt and pepper.

5   Add the butter to the pan and pour in the eggs. Use a spatula or wooden spoon to gently stir the eggs as they cook.

6   Once the eggs are forming lovely clumps and are still quite moist, which will take a couple of minutes, spoon directly on to the sourdough. Serve immediately, sprinkled with chopped chives.

Back when my husband David and I used to work together at Le Gavroche – one of the world's most celebrated French restaurants – we used to nip around the corner to a simple little café and order a croque monsieur for lunch. I've always told my French husband that this classic French dish is really just posh ham and cheese on toast, and the name stuck in our family. My favourite take is indulgent and rich, and works just as well later in the day with a lightly dressed salad. *Bon appétit*!

POSH HAM & CHEESE ON TOAST

SERVES 4

500ml milk

50g unsalted butter

50g plain flour

1 tablespoon Dijon mustard

300g Cheddar cheese, grated

4 sourdough bread slices

olive oil

100g Parma ham slices

1   Heat the milk in a saucepan.

2   In a separate saucepan, melt the butter and whisk in the flour. Whisk in the hot milk and continue whisking as the sauce comes to the boil, then cook for 2 minutes to cook out the flour.

3   Take off the heat and stir in the mustard and most of the Cheddar, reserving 80g.

4   Preheat the oven on the grill function.

5   Drizzle the sourdough with olive oil and blast one side under the grill.

6   Spread some of the cheese sauce over the sourdough on the untoasted sides and add a layer of the ham. Cover with the remaining sauce and then sprinkle over the reserved Cheddar.

7   Place the slices on a baking tray, then place back under the grill to melt the cheese. Serve immediately.

This is such a great way to share an omelette – you cook it in a large pan and place it right in the middle of the table so that everyone can tuck in. It's a different take on Omelette Arnold Bennett that uses flaked hot-smoked salmon instead of the usual smoked haddock. This version is now one of Papy's favourites (Papy is my husband David's very discerning father), so it must be good.

OPEN SMOKED SALMON OMELETTE

SERVES 4–6

6 large eggs
60g unsalted butter
4 hot-smoked salmon slices, flaked
100g Cheddar cheese, grated
toasted sourdough bread, to serve

FOR THE QUICK BÉCHAMEL

450ml milk
50g unsalted butter
50g plain flour
1 tablespoon Dijon mustard

1   To make the béchamel, heat the milk in a saucepan.

2   In a separate saucepan, melt the butter and whisk in the flour. Whisk the hot milk into the melted butter and flour and continue whisking as the sauce comes to the boil, then cook for 2 minutes to cook out the flour.

3   Take off the heat and stir in the mustard.

4   Preheat the oven on the grill function.

5   Break the eggs into bowl and beat lightly with a fork.

6   Heat a large nonstick frying pan over a medium heat. Add the butter and pour in the eggs. Cook the eggs gently, drawing the sides into the centre.

7   While the omelette is still quite runny, top with the flaked salmon, then pour over the béchamel to cover.

8   Sprinkle over the Cheddar, then place under the grill until the top is nice and golden. Serve immediately with some toasted sourdough.

We used to buy these biscuits in freshly made bundles in Samoa and they are very moreish. This version is not very sweet – I prefer them like this, but you can always add a little more sugar if you want. Traditionally served alongside a cup of tea or hot cocoa to dip into, they are also great on their own at any time. I like them in the morning for breakfast with yogurt and fruit, or later in the day served alongside a dessert.

MASI SAMOA – SAMOAN SHORTBREAD

MAKES 12

250g plain flour

1 teaspoon baking powder

pinch of salt

60g caster sugar, plus extra for dusting

100g coconut oil

125ml coconut milk (if using canned, shake the can before opening)

1   Preheat the oven to 170°C fan, Gas Mark 5.

2   Sift the flour, baking powder and salt together into a bowl.

3   Stir in the sugar and rub in the coconut oil with your fingers to a crumb.

4   Add the coconut milk and knead into a dough.

5   Place the dough between 2 sheets of nonstick baking paper and roll out into a 20cm square about 5mm thick. Cut into bars about 7 x 5cm, then place on a baking tray.

6   Bake for 30 minutes or until a nice golden brown. Dust with caster sugar while still warm, then cool completely on a wire rack. Store in an airtight container for up to 4 days.

We all know what it's like, rushing home midweek to make dinner.

'What's in the fridge?'

'Am I really hungry?'

'Do I need to eat?'

The answer to all these questions is: yes!

It's rare in our household that all three of us are at home to eat together in the evening due to the industry that my husband David and I work in, so we tend to opt for quick meals to save us spending hours in the kitchen preparing dinner. However, we all get involved – from setting the table to choosing the playlist we cook to.

WEEKNIGHTS

CONTENTS

Why spring onions? Well, simply because my daughter just LOVES them. It's wonderful to have a pile of these little fritters on the table, along with a chilled glass of wine. If spring onions aren't your thing, this batter recipe will work with many other vegetables and proteins as well – try it with anything from sliced courgettes and peppers, to prawns and strips of chicken. If you're using ingredients that take longer to cook, drop the temperature of the oil to 165°C so that they don't burn before they are cooked through.

SPRING ONION TEMPURA WITH SOY & GARLIC DIPPING SAUCE

SERVES 4–6

100g cornflour

100g plain flour

10g baking powder

pinch of salt and pepper

about 200ml sparkling water

400ml rapeseed oil

3 bunches of spring onions or about 5 per person, trimmed and outer layer peeled off, cut in half lengthways if thick

FOR THE DIPPING SAUCE

200ml soy sauce

juice of ½ lime

1 tablespoon mirin

½ tablespoon sesame oil

1 garlic clove, finely grated or chopped

1 tablespoon chopped red chilli
(I like my sauce hot so I keep the seeds in, but remove them if you prefer)

1 For the dipping sauce, mix all the ingredients together in a serving dish and set aside.

2 Mix the dry ingredients together in a bowl and make a well in the centre. Gradually pour in enough of the sparkling water while whisking until you have a thick batter (you may not need all the water).

3 Heat the rapeseed oil in a deep saucepan to 180°C (make sure the pan is no more than one-third full with oil).

4 Dip one of the spring onions into the batter to check it has a good coating consistency – add a little more water if necessary.

5 Coat the spring onions in the batter and fry in batches until golden, stirring to keep them from sticking together. Drain on kitchen paper, then serve while still hot with the dipping sauce.

Weeknights in our house are dictated by how hungry my daughter Anais is, and how exhausted my husband David and I feel. Something on toast – and a glass of wine for the grown-ups – is often the solution. This is one of our family's go-to standards for a meal that takes just minutes to prepare and is also utterly delicious! It works equally well with canned tuna chunks in place of the crab – use whichever you prefer. And of course, if you'd rather use your favourite shop-bought mayonnaise instead of making it from scratch, I won't mind at all.

CRAB & AVOCADO MASH-UP

SERVES 4–6

3 ripe avocados

10 cherry tomatoes, quartered

200g white crab meat

2 spring onions, finely sliced

50g Mayonnaise (see below)

5–6 drops of Tabasco sauce, or to taste

½ teaspoon Worcestershire sauce

4 sourdough bread slices

extra virgin olive oil

salt and pepper

FOR THE MAYONNAISE (MAKES 300G)

2 egg yolks

1 teaspoon Dijon mustard

1 tablespoon white wine vinegar

200ml rapeseed oil

lemon juice, to taste

1 For the mayonnaise, whisk the egg yolks, mustard and vinegar together in a bowl for 2 minutes.

2 Add the rapeseed oil while whisking continuously, very slowly at first, until fully emulsified.

3 Season with lemon juice, salt and pepper. Adjust the consistency with a bit of water if it's too thick. This can now be stored in a sterilized airtight jar (see page 17) in the refrigerator for up to a week.

4 Cut the avocados in half and remove the stones. Scrape the flesh out into a bowl and mash with a fork. Mix the cherry tomatoes through the avocado.

5 Fold in the crab and the spring onions, then the mayonnaise. Season with the Tabasco, then add the Worcestershire sauce, salt and pepper and fold through. Keep chilled until needed.

6 Preheat a griddle pan over a medium-high heat.

7 Drizzle the sourdough with extra virgin olive oil, and char on the hot griddle pan on both sides.

8 Spoon a generous amount of the crab and avocado mixture on the sourdough. Drizzle with olive oil and finish with a few twists of black pepper before serving.

I have only ever had poke one way in the Pacific Islands, so I'm not a fan of all the different poke takes out there. It's also one of the few dishes where I enjoy eating tuna, since I don't like cooked tuna. In Samoa, we use the freshest-caught tuna, cut into steaks and very simply prepared, served with sea grapes and washed down with the juice of a freshly picked coconut! I've also served this with the mashed avocado mixture from the Crab & Avocado Mash-Up (see page 44) underneath.

TUNA POKE

SERVES 4–6

1kg fresh tuna loin

FOR THE DRESSING

120ml dark soy sauce, or more to taste (I use Kikkoman)

2 tablespoons honey, or more to taste

1 tablespoon sesame oil

4 spring onions, finely sliced

2 garlic cloves, finely grated or chopped

2 tablespoons sesame seeds, toasted in a dry frying pan

2 teaspoons finely chopped red chilli, or more to taste

1   Mix all the dressing ingredients in a bowl. You can add extra soy sauce, honey or chilli to taste (the honey and soy needs to be balanced – not too sweet or too salty).

2   Cut the tuna into 1.5cm cubes.

3   Toss the tuna through the dressing and chill for 15 minutes before serving.

These absolutely hit the spot on a weeknight – savoury yet slightly sweet from the corn kernels, and very satisfying indeed. Although I've specified fresh corn, Mum used to make these with frozen corn, so use whichever you prefer. The horseradish cream will work with other dishes too – I've even folded it into a bowl of hot pasta sprinkled with bacon lardons.

SWEETCORN FRITTERS WITH HORSERADISH CREAM

SERVES 4–6

3 fresh corn on the cob

210g self-raising flour

2 eggs

60ml milk

2 egg whites

rapeseed oil

knob of butter (optional)

salt and pepper

FOR THE HORSERADISH CREAM

300g soured cream

2 tablespoons horseradish sauce

1 tablespoon chopped chives

2 pinches of salt

grated zest and juice of ½ unwaxed lemon

1 For the horseradish cream, mix all the ingredients together in a bowl. Correct the seasoning to taste. Keep chilled until needed.

2 Slice the corn kernels off the cobs and place in a bowl with the flour. Mix in the whole eggs and milk, then season with a pinch of salt and pepper.

3 In a separate bowl, whisk the egg whites to soft peaks using an electric hand whisk, then fold into the fritter mixture.

4 Heat a frying pan and add a little oil and a knob of butter, if you like.

5 Using a tablespoon, scoop and dollop the mixture into the hot pan to form separate rounds. Fry over a medium-low heat until golden brown on both sides. Serve warm with the horseradish cream.

Sometimes all I want is a cup of soup. Pea soup is one of my favourites, and peas are also one of the easiest vegetables to transform into a delicious soup in almost no time at all. If you want to make this a more substantial dish (as the others in my household prefer – otherwise they see it as just a drink!), serve it with poached eggs and croutons made from day-old bread.

PEA & COCONUT SOUP

SERVES 4–6

1 small onion, sliced

2 garlic cloves, sliced

2cm piece of fresh root ginger, peeled and sliced

1 tablespoon coconut oil

1kg frozen peas

400ml vegetable stock

300ml coconut milk

salt and pepper

1   Sweat the onion with the garlic and ginger in the coconut oil in a saucepan until soft, but without colouring.

2   Add the peas and cover with the vegetable stock, then add a few pinches of salt and a couple of twists of pepper.

3   Bring to the boil, then reduce the heat to a simmer and cook for 5 minutes.

4   Add the coconut milk. Pour the mixture into a blender and blitz until smooth, then serve.

Several times a year, my in-laws – known as Nany and Papy in our house – come from their home in the Jura in France to stay with us in London, especially to spend time with my daughter Anais. We've almost come to expect, when we get home after a day at work when Nany and Papy are here, that Nany will have made a batch of her legendary courgette soup, so we are quite disappointed at times when we get back to find that there isn't any! Her secret ingredient is cream cheese, used instead of cream. It's so simple and very delicious.

NANY'S COURGETTE SOUP

SERVES 4-6

1 onion, sliced

3 garlic cloves, sliced

olive oil

6 courgettes, grated

600ml vegetable stock

200g full-fat cream cheese, such as Philadelphia

½ lemon, for squeezing

salt and pepper

TO SERVE

crusty bread

1 garlic clove, peeled

1 Sweat the onion and garlic in a little olive oil in a saucepan over a medium heat for 2–3 minutes.

2 Set aside 4 tablespoons of the grated courgettes, then add the rest to the pan and stir for 2 minutes. Season with a little salt and pepper.

3 Add the vegetable stock and bring to the boil, then reduce the heat to a simmer and cook for 10–15 minutes. Stir in the cream cheese.

4 You can serve the soup like this or blitz in a blender for a smooth and rich result.

5 Season the reserved courgette with a pinch of salt and pepper, a squeeze of lemon juice and a drizzle of olive oil. Place a pile in the centre of each serving bowl and pour the soup around. Serve with crusty bread rubbed with a garlic clove and toasted.

This is a nice quick recipe we like to knock out when the barbecue is on, and we live off the barbecue in the summertime, so this recipe gets made quite often! We also find this a good way to get Anais eating mushrooms when she says she doesn't like them. Have the beetroot mixture and goats' cheese ready to go once the mushrooms are cooked.

PORTOBELLO MUSHROOMS, GOATS' CHEESE, BEETROOT & WALNUTS

SERVES 4-6

4 large Portobello mushrooms

olive oil

4 small beetroot, cooked in water for about 30 minutes until tender, then peeled and cut into small cubes (alternatively use ready-cooked beetroot, not in vinegar)

handful of walnut halves, toasted and broken up

2 tablespoons chopped flat leaf parsley

½ lemon, for squeezing

extra virgin olive oil

1 garlic clove, grated

1 tablespoon chopped chives

100g soft goats' cheese, such as La Buchette

1 tablespoon roughly chopped pickled walnuts

salt and pepper

1   Preheat the oven to 180°C fan, Gas Mark 6, and preheat a griddle pan over a high heat, if you don't have the barbecue going.

2   Drizzle the portobellos with olive oil and season with salt and pepper. Place on the hot griddle pan or barbecue and cook for 2 minutes on each side. Transfer to a baking tray and cook in the oven for 10 minutes.

3   Preheat the oven on the grill function.

4   Meanwhile, place the beetroot, toasted walnuts and parsley in a bowl. Add a few drops of lemon juice and 2 tablespoons extra virgin olive oil. Add the garlic and chives and toss everything together to coat well.

5   Spoon the beetroot mixture on top of the cooked mushrooms. Roughly break up the goats' cheese and sprinkle over the top.

6   Place under the hot grill (or place back on the barbecue) until the cheese begins to melt. Scatter the pickled walnuts on top to serve.

Cooking with my daughter Anais is a treasured part of my life, as I don't get to spend as much time with her as I'd like to. So a weeknight together is about the best quality time I can imagine, and an opportunity to teach her life lessons in the kitchen. This is, to date, her favourite curry recipe, and one we created together so it's very special to me. I'm not a massive rice fan – not since I had to eat it every day back in the Pacific Islands – but my husband David and Anais love it, so serve it alongside if you like.

ANAIS'S QUICK CHICKEN CURRY

SERVES 4–6

1 onion, finely chopped

2 garlic cloves, thinly sliced

2cm piece of fresh root ginger, peeled and grated

olive oil

1 teaspoon ground turmeric

1 teaspoon cumin seeds

1 teaspoon crushed coriander seeds

1 teaspoon chilli flakes or powder

500g boneless, skinless chicken thighs, cut into bite-sized chunks

2 sweet potatoes, peeled and cut into small chunks

1 butternut squash, peeled, deseeded and cut into small chunks

1 small cauliflower, cut into florets, stalk peeled and cut into cubes

500ml chicken stock

4 tablespoons Greek yogurt

salt

freshly chopped coriander, to serve

1   Sweat the onion, garlic and ginger in a little olive oil in a large saucepan until nice and caramelized.

2   Add the spices and cook for 2–3 minutes, stirring well, then add the chicken and season with a few twists of salt. Stir well to seal the chicken and cover in the spice mix.

3   Add all the vegetables and stir well.

4   Pour in the chicken stock and stir. Bring to the boil, then reduce the heat and simmer for 10 minutes, stirring now and then.

5   Stir in the Greek yogurt, then sprinkle with some freshly chopped coriander. Serve with rice or flatbreads.

This recipe is a take on a dish my Mum used to make. She would place all the chicken in a baking tray and cook it in the oven (there was a lot of it – we were a household of seven), then serve it with plain rice. The smell of the garlic and soy while it was cooking would draw me out of my bedroom. Pak choi is the perfect green accompaniment – we always had a lot of it because my Dad grew it in his vast and sprawling vegetable garden (he grows everything, everywhere!) – and it has been one of my favourite vegetables for as long as I can remember.

SOY & HONEY CHICKEN WITH COCONUT RICE

SERVES 4

100g honey
150ml dark soy sauce
8 boneless, skinless chicken thighs
handful of coriander, chopped

FOR THE COCONUT RICE

150g brown rice
2 pinches of salt
300ml water
1 teaspoon coconut oil
1 teaspoon sesame seeds
1 teaspoon chopped pumpkin seeds

FOR THE PAK CHOI

1 tablespoon sesame oil
1 tablespoon rapeseed oil
8 baby pak choi, cut in half lengthways
1 garlic clove, thinly sliced
salt and pepper

1 Mix the honey and soy sauce together in a bowl, add the chicken thighs and turn to coat all over.

2 Transfer the chicken to a heavy-based saucepan, scraping in all the sticky honey marinade.

3 Place the pan over a medium heat and cook for 10 minutes, turning halfway, until the chicken is cooked and the honey and soy coating has thickened to a glossy glaze. (It's important to start with a cold pan so the chicken stews in the liquid as it cooks; if your pan is too hot it will seal the chicken and caramelize the honey and soy too quickly, turning it bitter before the meat is cooked.)

4 While the chicken is cooking, place the rice in a saucepan and add the salt and water. Bring to the boil, then reduce the heat to a gentle simmer, cover and cook for about 20–25 minutes until tender and fluffy.

5 For the pak choi, heat the sesame and rapeseed oils in a pan over a medium heat. Add the pak choi and garlic, season with a little salt and pepper and cook for 3–4 minutes until tender.

6 When the rice is cooked, fluff with a fork and stir in the coconut oil and sesame seeds. Sprinkle the chopped pumpkin seeds on top.

7 Serve the chicken with the rice and the pak choi, and with the chopped coriander sprinkled over the top.

I love, love, love cauliflower in any form – roasted, grilled, steamed with flavoured butter – so for me this is one of my favourite salads. Serve either on its own, accompanying a meat or fish dish, or alongside whatever you're cooking on the barbecue. It's great with those smoky, charred flavours, so this is something we tend to eat often over the summer.

CAULIFLOWER COUSCOUS

SERVES 4–6

1 medium cauliflower

15 ready-to-eat dried apricots, cut into strips

2 tablespoons roughly chopped pistachio nuts

2 tablespoons roughly chopped flat leaf parsley

¼ teaspoon ground cumin

¼ teaspoon ground turmeric

½ lemon, for squeezing

2–3 tablespoons extra virgin olive oil

salt and pepper

1 Cut the cauliflower into chunks to fit into your food processor or blender.

2 Pulse to a couscous-like texture, scraping down the sides at intervals. Scrape the cauliflower into a bowl.

3 Add the apricots to the cauliflower with the pistachios and parsley. Add the spices and mix well.

4 Add a few drops of lemon juice and the extra virgin olive oil, then toss through the couscous to dress. Season to taste with salt and pepper.

Bulgur wheat is a staple in our house, and I prefer the coarse bulgur to the fine bulgur because of its texture. I like to sweat it off first in a hot pan, as it really enhances the nuttiness of the wheat. The addition of ras el hanout – a North African spice mix that's woody, pungent and slightly sweet – really makes this dish sing. When I was last in Morocco, I bought bags of it from a market where every spice merchant had their own version of the mix – every one different, all of them delicious.

BULGUR, FIGS & RAS EL HANOUT

SERVES 4-6

olive oil

250g bulgur wheat

1 tablespoon chopped rosemary leaves

1 tablespoon thyme leaves

250ml water

1 bunch of flat leaf parsley, roughly chopped

grated zest and juice of 1 unwaxed lemon

2 teaspoons ras el hanout

150g cucumber, peeled, deseeded and cut into cubes

6 dried figs, chopped

salt and pepper

1 Heat a nonstick saucepan over a medium heat and add a drizzle of olive oil.

2 Add the bulgur, rosemary and thyme and stir for 2 minutes. Season with a pinch of salt and a few twists of pepper.

3 Pour in the water and bring to the boil, then cover, turn off the heat and leave to sit until all the liquid has been absorbed.

4 Transfer to a bowl and fluff with a fork. Mix the parsley, lemon zest, ras el hanout, cucumber and figs through the bulgur, then squeeze over half the lemon juice.

5 Correct the seasoning to taste with salt and pepper and more lemon juice and olive oil if needed.

I love Marmite SO much – especially the version sold in New Zealand, which is much darker and not as bitter as the UK variety. And Marmite loves butter. Once a month is my Marmite day when I have four pieces of buttery toast with Marmite on top – heaven. And Marmite again for supper, with more butter alongside mushrooms and pasta! This is rich, satisfying and will work a treat with whatever mushrooms you have to hand.

MIXED MUSHROOM PASTA WITH MARMITE

SERVES 4-6

120g oyster mushrooms

100g baby chestnut mushroom

100g button mushrooms

olive oil

1 small onion, finely chopped

230g tagliatelle (fresh or dried)

120g unsalted butter

1 tablespoon Marmite

1 teaspoon honey

salt and pepper

freshly grated Parmesan cheese, to serve

1 Clean the mushrooms by wiping them with a damp tea towel or brushing.

2 Tear the oyster mushrooms into 2 or 3 pieces, depending on size. Trim the stalks on the chestnut and button mushrooms, then cut into quarters.

3 Heat a large nonstick frying pan with a few drops of olive oil.

4 Add the onion and sweat until soft but without colouring. Add the mushrooms and cook until golden.

5 Meanwhile, bring a large pan of water to the boil and add a few pinches of salt. Cook the pasta according to the packet instructions, then drain and set aside, reserving 200ml of the pasta cooking water.

6 Add the reserved pasta water to the mushroom mixture, then stir in the butter, Marmite and honey and simmer to form a sauce.

7 Add the pasta to the mushroom sauce and toss through to mix. Finish by seasoning with salt and pepper to taste and serve with some freshly grated Parmesan at the table.

Papy, my husband David's Dad, is our star tomato tart maker during holidays. He is so proud of this recipe, as it was the first thing he made that my daughter Anais demolished in one sitting when she was about five years old. He still loves making it for her when it's just the two of them, but of course (we hope!) saving some for David and me to eat when we get home. It needs no accompaniment: Papy serves it straight up, on its own.

PAPY'S TOMATO TART

SERVES 4

olive oil

2 bacon rashers, roughly chopped

1 onion, finely chopped

2 eggs

220ml milk

1 tablespoon finely chopped fresh oregano, if possible, or 1 teaspoon dried oregano

320g sheet of ready-rolled puff pastry

5 ripe tomatoes, sliced

salt and pepper

1 Preheat the oven to 190°C fan, Gas Mark 6½.

2 Heat a nonstick frying pan and add a drizzle of olive oil.

3 Fry the bacon, then add the onion and cook over a medium heat for 2 minutes. Leave to cool.

4 Beat the eggs and milk together in a bowl. Season with salt and pepper and add the oregano.

5 Take a baking tray, about 34 x 24cm and at least 2cm deep. Unroll the pastry into the tin and press it up the sides.

6 Spread the bacon and onion mixture over the pastry base, and cover with a layer of the tomato slices.

7 Pour over the egg mixture, then bake for 15–20 minutes until golden. Serve warm.

If you've never tried coffee on a salad, trust me and give it a go. A good friend of mine first introduced me to the idea, and I promise you that the bitterness of the coffee really gives this simple salad a lift. I love it on its own, but it's great as a side dish too. Try it alongside an oily fish such as salmon or mackerel, if you're after a more substantial meal.

FENNEL, ORANGE & KOHLRABI SALAD WITH COFFEE

SERVES 4

1 large fennel bulb
1 kohlrabi
2 oranges
grated zest and juice of 1 unwaxed lemon
about 50ml extra virgin olive oil
1 teaspoon instant coffee granules
salt and pepper

1   Finely slice or grate the fennel and place in a large bowl.

2   Peel then grate the kohlrabi, then mix with the fennel.

3   Zest the oranges into the bowl. Remove all the skin and pith from the oranges and cut the fruit into thin rounds.

4   Zest the lemon into the bowl and add the juice, then season with salt and pepper and the extra virgin olive oil. Toss gently with the orange rounds.

5   Grind the coffee granules to a powder with a spoon in a small bowl, then sprinkle over the salad and serve.

This is one of my favourite quick desserts – it's a hand-me-down recipe from a very dear family friend who is a fabulous cook. Pam is one of those amazing people whose house you never want to leave. She cooks everything from scratch, she's always happy to serve up another plate no matter how many people are there and she always has a pudding. I almost don't want to share this recipe, it's so good – perhaps I should just keep it to myself?

APPLE & BLACKBERRY BAKE

SERVES 4-6

200g soft unsalted butter

150g caster sugar

300g Bramley apples, peeled, cored and thickly sliced

2 pinches of ground cinnamon

1 punnet blackberries, about 160g

2 eggs

120g ground almonds

vanilla ice cream, to serve

1   Preheat the oven to 160°C fan, Gas Mark 4.

2   Spread 80g of the butter all over the base of a 26 x 20cm baking dish, then pour 60g of the sugar over the butter and give the dish a gentle shake to cover evenly.

3   Arrange the apple slices overlapping to cover the butter and sugar. Sprinkle over the cinnamon, then arrange the blackberries evenly over the apples.

4   Beat the remaining butter and sugar together in a bowl until pale and creamy. Beat in the eggs one at a time. Mix in the ground almonds, then spread the mixture over the fruit.

5   Bake for 45 minutes–1 hour until golden brown and starting to caramelize at the edges.

6   Leave to sit for 10 minutes before serving with a scoop of your favourite vanilla ice cream.

This dessert is another recipe that was handed down to me by an Aunty, and I like to serve it with lashings of custard (though it's just fine on its own, too). Instead of the jam, which can be whatever flavour you prefer, I also like to use stewed fruit – any ripe fruit from your fruit bowl will work well.

A QUICK MIDWEEK PUDDING

SERVES 4

90g stale breadcrumbs

2 large eggs, separated

400ml milk

¼ teaspoon vanilla bean paste

85g caster sugar

5 tablespoons apricot jam or your favourite flavour

1   Preheat the oven to 170°C fan, Gas Mark 5.

2   Spread the breadcrumbs in the base of a 25 x 16cm baking dish.

3   Beat the egg yolks, milk, vanilla and 30g of the sugar together in a bowl and pour over the breadcrumbs.

4   Bake for 20–25 minutes or until set and cooked through. Leave to cool, then spread the jam over the top.

5   Increase the oven temperature to 190°C fan, Gas Mark 6½.

6   Whisk the egg whites to soft peaks using an electric hand whisk, then gradually whisk in the remaining sugar and spread over the pudding.

7   Return the pudding to the oven and bake for about 10 minutes or until it starts turning golden.

Sunday is the day we always look forward to – a real family day, and very much cherished since we're all so busy during the week. Sunday is the only day that we close the restaurant, so it's also our opportunity to catch up with good friends. And to be honest, with no 'real' family nearby except the three of us, our good friends in the UK have become a part of our family, too.

We tend to plan at least a few days ahead – thinking about what the weather might be like, what's in season and, of course, asking the boss (aka my daughter Anais!) what she'd like to eat. Getting the ingredients assembled, gathering a few friends and cooking, laughing and eating all together with no fixed agenda – sounds like a perfect Sunday to me.

THE PERFECT SUNDAY

CONTENTS

I do love a glass of something delicious while we're bringing a meal together on a Sunday – and it's good to have something to nibble alongside, otherwise it's a slippery slope! We always enjoy these nuts during our pre-dinner drinks, and they're also great for entertaining. You can use whichever nuts, herbs and spices you prefer.

LEMON THYME & HONEY SPICED NUTS

SERVES 4-6

100g cashew nuts

100g pistachio nuts

100g walnuts

100g honey

2 tablespoons finely chopped lemon thyme leaves

1 tablespoon finely chopped rosemary leaves

1 teaspoon smoked paprika

½ teaspoon sea salt flakes

1   Preheat the oven to 180°C fan, Gas Mark 6.

2   Place all the ingredients in a bowl and mix to coat the nuts.

3   Pour on to a large baking tray, then roast for 15 minutes or until golden brown, stirring now and then.

4   Leave to cool, then break apart and serve in bowls with your favourite aperitif. These will store in an airtight container for up 3 days.

Morteau sausages are a smoked variety typically from the town of Morteau in France, and they are my husband's favourite. We always have some in the freezer. You can use a different type of smoked sausage instead, such as smoked salami or chorizo, and 'nduja from Italy also works well here. If you're planning to serve these with pre-dinner drinks (and I recommend that you do), use the smallest potatoes you can find.

CRISPY MORTEAU & CHEESE-FILLED POTATOES

SERVES 4–6

coarse rock salt

10 Ratte or baby potatoes, washed and patted dry

100g Morteau sausage

olive oil

1 small soft cheese, such as Vacherin Mont d'Or or goats' cheese

FOR THE PICKLED SHALLOTS

100ml water

100ml white wine vinegar

50g sugar

1 banana shallot, sliced

1 Preheat the oven to 165°C fan, Gas Mark 4.

2 Sprinkle a layer of rock salt on a baking tray and place the whole potatoes on top. Bake the potatoes for about 40 minutes until cooked through, then leave to cool but leave the oven on. Once the salt has cooled, you can store it in a container to be reused.

3 While the potatoes are baking, cook the sausage whole in a pan of simmering water for 40 minutes, then leave to cool in the water.

4 Meanwhile, for the pickled shallots, simmer the water, vinegar and sugar in a saucepan until the sugar has dissolved. Add the sliced shallot and leave to cool in the liquid for at least 5 minutes.

5 Cut the cooled potatoes in half lengthways and scoop out most of the potato flesh into a large bowl. Sit the potato shells on the baking tray, drizzle lightly with olive oil and return to the oven for 20 minutes until golden brown.

6 Peel and discard the skin from the cooled sausage, then cut the sausage meat into small dice and add to the potato flesh.

7 Drain the pickled shallot and add it to the bowl, stir everything to combine, then press the mixture into the potato shells.

8 Place a spoonful of the cheese on top of each, then return to the oven and cook for 7–10 minutes to reheat and melt the cheese.

There's always a salad on our table either at lunch or dinner or both, especially in the summer months. I like texture and flavour bursts in my salads so that they're more interesting and not just dull and leafy, which also helps get my daughter excited about them. Have fun with them and use whatever alternative herbs, nuts or fruits you fancy – peaches and watermelon are worth a try too.

WALNUT, BLACKBERRY & FETA SALAD

SERVES 4

300g sourdough bread

good-quality olive oil

1 punnet of blackberries, about 150g

8 walnut halves, toasted

1 Granny Smith apple, cored and cut into small chunks

2 spring onions, sliced

1 red chilli, finely sliced

3 dill sprigs, shredded

8 mint leaves, shredded

2 Little Gem lettuces, bases trimmed and shredded

80g feta cheese

salt and pepper

FOR THE VINAIGRETTE

100ml extra virgin olive oil

1 tablespoon cider vinegar

1 tablespoon wholegrain mustard

1 tablespoon honey

1   For the vinaigrette, whisk all the ingredients together in a bowl and set aside.

2   Preheat the oven to 180°C fan, Gas Mark 6.

3   To make croutons, tear the sourdough into bite-sized pieces, place on a baking tray and drizzle with a little olive oil. Bake for 10 minutes, stirring now and then, until crispy. Set them aside to cool.

4   Meanwhile, put the blackberries, walnut halves, apple, spring onions, chilli, herbs and lettuce into a large serving bowl. Season with a little salt and pepper.

5   Toss the croutons through the vinaigrette, pour over the salad and gently toss everything together.

6   Break up the feta over the top of the salad and serve.

I absolutely adore beetroot in all shapes and sizes – I even grow them when possible. This salt crust recipe works wonderfully with all root vegetables as well as meats. If you don't have time to bake the beetroot, use ready-cooked ones. The salt dough can be kept in the fridge for up to 5 days – just remember to get it out 30 minutes before you use it so that it's easier to roll out.

SALT-BAKED BEETROOT SALAD

SERVES 4-6

8 small red beetroot, washed and patted dry

8 small yellow beetroot, washed and patted dry

2 garlic cloves, peeled

½ lemon, for squeezing

80ml extra virgin olive oil

handful of flat leaf parsley, shredded

80g feta cheese (optional)

salt and pepper

FOR THE SALT DOUGH

500g plain flour

300g rock salt

100g fine salt

4 rosemary sprigs, chopped

3 thyme sprigs, chopped

1 teaspoon dried lavender flowers

3 large egg whites (100g in total)

150ml water

1   For the salt dough, mix the flour, salts and herbs together in a bowl. Mix in the egg whites, then add the water and knead the mixture together in the bowl to form a dough.

2   Preheat the oven to 170°C fan, Gas Mark 5.

3   Place the beetroot on a large baking tray.

4   Roll out the salt dough on a floured work surface to about 5mm thick.

5   Cover the tray and beetroot with the salt dough like a pie and press down to mould it over the beetroot, then bake for 1 hour.

6   Remove the tray from the oven and leave to cool until just warm, then remove and discard the crust and peel the beetroot. Cut the beetroot into bite-sized pieces and place in a bowl.

7   Grate in the garlic cloves. Add a squeeze of lemon juice, the olive oil and the parsley. Season with salt and pepper and toss everything together.

8   If using, crumble the feta over the top before serving.

By now it's no secret how much I enjoy Marmite, but this is a great bread even without it, so if you're not a Marmite lover, just leave it out. Focaccia is a delight for pre-dinner drinks and there are countless toppings you can use if you want to add an extra touch – try mozzarella, Cheddar, halved green olives or sliced tomatoes – you can almost treat it like a thick pizza base. This is also great as a side dish to accompany other dishes. Should you want to prepare it in advance, make the dough the day before and refrigerate it overnight, then take it out and leave it for 30 minutes before knocking it back gently and pressing it into your baking tin.

ROSEMARY & MARMITE FOCACCIA

SERVES 4–6 AS A
PRE-DINNER DISH

10g Marmite

5g fresh yeast, crumbled, or fast-action dried yeast

175ml warm water

250g strong white flour

5g salt

extra virgin olive oil

1 rosemary sprig, leaves picked and chopped

sea salt flakes

1   Whisk the Marmite and yeast into the warm water until dissolved.

2   Mix the flour and salt together in a bowl and make a well in the centre.

3   Pour the yeast mixture into the flour and gradually mix in to form a dough, then knead into a firm ball. Place in a large bowl and drizzle over some extra virgin olive oil. Cover and leave in a warm place for 1½–2 hours or until doubled in size.

4   Press the dough into a 28 x 20cm shallow baking tin, cover and leave in a warm place for about 45 minutes until doubled in size.

5   Preheat the oven to 180°C fan, Gas Mark 6.

6   Use your fingers to gently push indents into the dough. Liberally drizzle extra virgin olive oil all over the surface, then sprinkle with the rosemary and some sea salt flakes.

7   Bake for 25–30 minutes until golden brown. Cut into squares and serve warm.

Crumpets, yum! These are the product of an experiment to find a cornbread of sorts that I could serve with a dish at the restaurant. Of course, they can be made plain without the corn, but it's a fantastic addition and we've come to love them this way. When we make a batch, we always bake extra and then freeze them, so that on busy days we can just pop them straight from the freezer into the toaster. This is definitely a great one for when my daughter Anais has friends staying over and we put out a selection of toppings for them, from berries to golden syrup and butter.

SWEETCORN CRUMPETS

MAKES 20

100g fresh or frozen sweetcorn kernels

20g caster sugar

10g fresh yeast, crumbled, or fast-action dried yeast

125g strong white flour

125g plain flour

5g salt

1 teaspoon baking powder

nonstick cooking spray

rapeseed oil

1 Cook the sweetcorn in a large pan of unsalted boiling water for 2–3 minutes, then drain, reserving 375ml of the cooking water. Roughly chop the sweetcorn.

2 Set aside 75ml of the reserved cooking water. Leave the remaining 300ml water to cool until warm, then whisk in the sugar and yeast.

3 Mix the flours and salt together in a bowl and make a well in the centre. Pour the yeast mixture into the flour and whisk in until well combined. Cover and leave in a warm place for about 30 minutes until doubled in size.

4 Whisk the 75ml reserved cooking water and baking powder together and add to the batter. Fold in the chopped sweetcorn.

5 Spray 4 metal crumpet/egg rings, 8.5–9cm in diameter, with nonstick cooking spray.

6 Heat a large frying pan over a gentle heat and add a little oil.

7 Place the rings in the pan, then fill each ring one-third full with the batter and cook until bubbles appear on the surface (the batter should double in size as it cooks).

8 Remove the rings, flip the crumpets over and cook until golden on the underside and just firm to touch. Repeat with the remaining batter, adding a little more oil as needed. Serve warm or, if made in advance, toast before serving.

Cheese scones were such a treat growing up. Mum used to toast them, and we'd then slather them with butter. This is still how I prefer them, so I'm pleased that my daughter now enjoys them the same way, too. You can shape this dough into individual scones, though I like it as a loaf so that I can just cut slices and pop them into the toaster!

PARMESAN SCONE LOAF

MAKES 12 SLICES

250g plain flour, plus extra for dusting

15g baking powder

1 teaspoon cayenne pepper

¼ teaspoon salt

60g cold unsalted butter, diced, plus extra for greasing

100g Parmesan cheese, grated

125ml milk

2 teaspoons olive oil

1 egg

1 Preheat the oven to 180°C fan, Gas Mark 6, and grease a 24 x 14cm loaf tin.

2 Sift the flour, baking powder and cayenne together into a bowl. Stir in the salt, then rub in the butter to form a crumb.

3 Set aside a handful of the Parmesan, then add the rest to the scone mixture and mix it in.

4 Beat the milk, olive oil and egg together, then pour into the scone mixture and quickly bring together to form a dough.

5 Turn the dough out on to a lightly floured work surface. Press into a rectangular slab about 3cm thick and place in the prepared tin.

6 Sprinkle the reserved Parmesan on top, then bake for 30 minutes or until golden. Cool on a wire rack and store in an airtight container for up to 3 days.

Spätzle is actually so easy to make – quicker than making pasta and a great alternative – so I recommend you give it a go. Once cooled and drained, you can drizzle with olive oil and it will keep in the fridge for up to 3 days. I also love plain spätzle sautéed in a little oil until golden before adding to the rest of a dish, as well as cooked this way and served on its own as a side dish.

CHICKEN & MUSHROOM SPÄTZLE

SERVES 4–6

olive oil

100g bacon lardons

4 boneless, skinless chicken thighs, cut into strips

1 garlic clove, thinly sliced

1 punnet of button mushrooms, about 200g, halved

70g unsalted butter

salt and pepper

FOR THE SPÄTZLE

170g plain flour

2 pinches of salt

1 teaspoon finely chopped thyme leaves

1 teaspoon finely chopped rosemary leaves

3 eggs

1 tablespoon olive oil

TO SERVE

1 tablespoon chopped rosemary leaves

Parmesan cheese shavings

1 For the spätzle, mix the flour, salt and herbs together in a bowl and make a well in the centre.

2 Beat the eggs and olive oil lightly together, then pour into the flour mixture and whisk to make a thick batter.

3 Take a colander and sit it on top of a deep saucepan of boiling water. Ladle the batter into the colander, and use the base of the ladle to press the batter so that it drops through the holes into the boiling water. As the spätzle float to the surface, use a slotted spoon to scoop them into a sieve. Reserve 300ml of the spätzle cooking water.

4 Refresh the spätzle in iced water, then drain.

5 Heat a nonstick saucepan over a medium heat and add a little olive oil. Add the lardons and cook until golden, then add the chicken strips and cook until golden.

6 Add the garlic and cook for 2 minutes, stirring, then add the mushrooms and cook for 3 minutes until golden. Add the butter and cook until it starts to foam.

7 Pour in half of the reserved spätzle cooking water and bring to a simmer for 5 minutes, stirring.

8 Add the spätzle and the remaining cooking water, if needed, and return to a simmer. Season with salt and pepper, sprinkle with chopped rosemary and serve immediately with some Parmesan shavings on top.

These are such a tasty treat that you'll need to be quick to get in before they all disappear! The potato mixture can also be formed into small balls and pressed flat to serve with drinks, but I find these full-sized ones much more satisfyingly indulgent. It's also a great way to use up any leftover baked potatoes.

CHORIZO & CHEESE POTATO MELTS

SERVES 4

4 large potatoes (such as Maris Piper or Désirée), peeled and cut into chunks

40g plain flour

½ teaspoon paprika

½ teaspoon ground cumin

2 pinches each of salt and pepper

2 eggs

12 thin cooked chorizo slices

80g Brie cheese, cut into 4

rapeseed oil

100g unsalted butter

mustard, to serve

1 Cook the potatoes in a pan of salted boiling water for 10–15 minutes until tender. Drain well, then return to the pan and leave to dry out for a few minutes before mashing.

2 Mix in the flour, spices, the salt and pepper and eggs.

3 Divide the potato mixture into 8 equal amounts, then place on a baking tray lined with greaseproof paper. Flatten and shape the mixture into 8cm squares.

4 Place 3 slices of chorizo and a piece of cheese on 4 of the potato squares. Cover them with the remaining potato squares to make a sandwich, then gently press the edges together to seal in the filling. Chill for 30 minutes until firm.

5 When you are ready to cook, use a flat spatula to square off the sides neatly.

6 Add a little oil and the butter to a frying pan and heat until foaming. Add the potato cakes and fry over a medium heat, turning, until golden brown on both sides. Serve hot with a little mustard on the side.

This is one of our favourites from New Zealand, where you can find bacon and egg pies in almost every café or deli. I like mine finished with smoked paprika and will sometimes add tomatoes when we have them – simply cut in half and placed on top.

BACON & EGG PIE

SERVES 4–6

14 streaky bacon rashers, each cut into thirds

1 small onion, chopped

rapeseed oil, if needed

8 eggs

smoked paprika, for seasoning

200ml double cream

2 tablespoons chopped chives

1 egg yolk, beaten with a little water, for glazing

salt

FOR THE SHORTCRUST PASTRY

400g plain flour, plus extra for dusting

2 pinches of salt

250g cold unsalted butter, diced, plus extra for greasing

3 tablespoons water

1   To make the pastry, mix the flour and salt together in a bowl, then rub in the butter to form a crumb. Mix in the water to form a dough. Shape into a ball, wrap and chill for 30 minutes.

2   Preheat the oven to 200°C fan, Gas Mark 7.

3   Heat a large frying pan and quickly fry the bacon (alternatively, place it on a baking tray and cook in the oven for 2–3 minutes). Set aside and leave to cool.

4   Fry the onion for a few minutes until lightly coloured, then leave to cool.

5   Grease a shallow baking tin about 20cm square.

6   On a lightly floured work surface, roll out the pastry into 2 sheets each about 5mm thick, one large enough to line the tin and the other for the pie lid.

7   Line the greased tin with the first pastry sheet.

8   Add the cooled bacon and onion in a layer over the base, then crack in 7 of the eggs evenly on top. Pierce the yolks, then lightly season with salt (remembering that the bacon is salty too) and a light sprinkling of smoked paprika.

9   Mix the cream with the remaining egg and the chives and pour over the eggs and bacon.

10   Place the second sheet of pastry on top to cover the pie, firmly pressing the edges together to seal and trimming any excess pastry. Use any trimmings to decorate the pie if you like, then brush the top with the egg and water mixture to glaze.

11   Bake for 30–40 minutes until nice and golden. Serve at room temperature.

Our household really enjoys offal, and lambs' kidneys are top of our list. And we're not alone – whenever I prepare them on television, viewers tell me how much they love them. We are fortunate to have a small family-run butcher nearby that always has some in stock, but if you can't find them, order from your nearest butcher.

LAMBS' KIDNEYS WITH TOMATO, TARRAGON & CAPERS

SERVES 4

olive oil

1 small onion, chopped

3 garlic cloves, 2 thinly sliced, 1 peeled but left whole

2 tablespoons tomato purée

400g can chopped tomatoes

1 tablespoon Worcestershire sauce

1 tablespoon fine capers

3 tarragon sprigs, chopped

16 lambs' kidneys, cleaned (you can usually buy them cleaned, or ask the butcher to do this for you)

4 sourdough bread slices

salt and pepper

1 Heat a nonstick saucepan and add a little olive oil. Add the onion and sliced garlic and cook over a medium heat until transparent. Stir in the tomato purée and cook for 2 minutes.

2 Add the chopped tomatoes and Worcestershire sauce. Season with a pinch of salt and a little pepper. Simmer gently for 10 minutes, stirring now and then.

3 Stir in the capers, then stir in tarragon and take off the heat.

4 Preheat a griddle pan over a medium-high heat.

5 Lightly season the kidneys and drizzle with a little olive oil. Cook for about 2 minutes on each side (depending on their size) for medium. Set aside.

6 Rub the sourdough with the remaining garlic clove, drizzle with olive oil and char on both sides on the hot griddle pan.

7 Serve the tomato sauce on the sourdough topped with the kidneys.

While roast pork shoulder is wonderful with crackling, we also enjoy this recipe with this delicious pistachio stuffing, which I like to make during the Christmas season. Sometimes I make a bigger batch of the stuffing, roll it up in foil and bake it separately, then serve it sliced on the side, especially when we have friends and family over and there are certain allergies or intolerances to cater for.

PORK SHOULDER WITH PISTACHIO STUFFING

SERVES 4–6

1.2kg boned and rolled pork shoulder joint

1 tablespoon honey

salt and pepper

FOR THE PISTACHIO STUFFING

1 shallot, chopped

1 garlic clove, sliced

olive oil

6 button mushrooms, chopped

20g pistachio nuts

1 tablespoon chopped flat leaf parsley

1 teaspoon chopped rosemary leaves

4 slightly stale bread slices, blitzed to crumbs

1 small egg

50ml milk

½ teaspoon ground nutmeg

1. For the stuffing, sweat the shallot and garlic in a little olive oil in a frying pan over a medium heat for 2 minutes. Add the mushrooms and cook until their juices have evaporated but without colouring, then set aside.

2. Meanwhile, blanch the pistachios in boiling water for 1 minute, then drain.

3. Mix the mushroom mixture, pistachios and herbs with the breadcrumbs in a bowl.

4. Beat the egg, milk and nutmeg together in a separate bowl and season with a little salt and a few twists of pepper. Add to the breadcrumb mixture and mix to bind.

5. Open up the pork shoulder and season the inside with salt and pepper.

6. Form the stuffing into a log shape, place in the seasoned pork shoulder, then roll up. Tie the rolled joint with butcher's string in the centre and at both ends to secure.

7. Score the skin of the pork with a sharp knife, then rub the honey all over.

8. Season the pork with salt and rub it in, then place in a large roasting tray and leave to sit at room temperature for 30 minutes.

9. Meanwhile, preheat the oven to 160°C fan, Gas Mark 4.

10. Roast the pork for 50 minutes, then increase the oven temperature to 180°C fan, Gas Mark 6, and roast for a further 20–30 minutes. Leave to rest for 10 minutes before serving.

With beautiful ingredients such as fresh fish, I like to keep things simple. Cooking on a barbecue brings great flavour to fish (as well as meats), and leaving it whole also means the fish will stay moist. When it's ready, set the whole fish on a platter in the middle of the table so that everyone can help themselves.

WHOLE GRILLED SEA BASS WITH SOY GARLIC DRESSING & SPRING ONIONS

SERVES 4-6

1 –1.2kg plus whole sea bass, scaled and gutted, at room temperature

1 lemon, sliced

½ bunch of coriander, roughly chopped

rapeseed oil

salt and pepper

FOR THE DRESSING

2cm piece of fresh root ginger, peeled and grated

2 garlic cloves, grated

2 spring onions, finely sliced

1 red chilli, finely sliced

50ml dark soy sauce

20ml mirin

1   Take the fish out of the refrigerator 10 minutes before you are ready to cook. Season the inside of the bass with salt and pepper and stuff with the lemon slices and coriander.

2   Preheat a barbecue. Alternatively, preheat a baking tray in the oven on the grill function at its highest setting.

3   Pat the fish dry on both sides as much as possible. Using a sharp knife, score the skin of the fish at intervals from the tail to the head on both sides and pat dry again.

4   Wipe or brush the barbecue (or baking tray) with oil to prevent the fish from sticking.

5   Place the fish on the barbecue, making sure it is on the hottest part, and cook for 4–5 minutes. Use 2 flat spatulas to lift and turn the fish, then cook on the other side for 4–5 minutes, by which time the skin should be nice and crispy. Alternatively, place the fish on the preheated baking tray and grill for 10–12 minutes or until cooked through.

6   While the fish is cooking, make the dressing. Place the ginger and garlic in a bowl with the spring onions and chilli. Add the soy and mirin and whisk together.

7   Pour the dressing over the fish when it comes off the barbecue and serve immediately.

Fish and chips is a definite must for us Galettis. Mushy peas were a revelation to me when I moved to the UK, and this quick take on them ticks the box in our household, especially when we decide to make them at the last minute and haven't left the dried peas to soak the day before. And the beer batter brings a fabulous flavour that takes the whole experience to another level!

BEER-BATTERED FISH & ROSEMARY SALT CHIPS

SERVES 4

230g self-raising flour

440ml can beer or lager – whatever is to hand

450ml rapeseed oil

4 large King Edwards or other floury potatoes, peeled and cut into chunky chips

4 haddock fillets, about 180g each

1 tablespoon sea salt flakes

2 tablespoons chopped rosemary leaves

FOR THE EASY MUSHY PEAS

250g frozen peas

1 tablespoon cider vinegar

40g unsalted butter

salt and pepper

1   For the mushy peas, bring the peas to the boil in a saucepan of water, then drain. Return the peas to the saucepan and mash with a fork. Mash in the vinegar and butter, then season to taste with salt and pepper. Keep warm while you cook the fish.

2   Place the flour in a large bowl and make a well in the centre. Gradually pour in the beer while whisking to make a thick batter.

3   Pour enough rapeseed oil to fry the fish and chips into a large, deep saucepan (make sure the pan is no more than one-third full with oil) or deep-fat fryer and heat to 165°C.

4   Fry the chips for 5 minutes to part-cook, then drain on kitchen paper.

5   Increase the oil temperature to 180°C.

6   Pat the fish dry, then dip into the batter to coat. Carefully drop the fish into the hot oil, one fillet at a time, and cook until golden on both sides. Drain on kitchen paper, and keep warm while you re-fry the chips, this time until golden.

7   Mix the salt flakes and rosemary together and use to season the chips before serving with the fish and mushy peas.

David, my husband, made these so often at one stage that we had to put a stop to it – we were eating a whole batch every week! His twist is to bake the brownie mixture in a loaf tin so that it can be served slice after slice. This recipe is best made with extra-bitter dark chocolate, and our favourite way to serve the brownies is just warm with a large scoop of vanilla ice cream.

LOCKDOWN BROWNIES

SERVES 6–8

220g unsalted butter, chopped

260g dark chocolate (70% cocoa), broken into pieces

320g caster sugar

200g plain flour, sifted

150g fudge pieces

5 eggs

1 teaspoon vanilla bean paste

½ teaspoon salt

vanilla ice cream, to serve

1   Preheat the oven to 170°C fan, Gas Mark 5. Line a 24 x 13cm loaf tin with nonstick baking paper.

2   Melt the butter and chocolate together in a large heatproof bowl over a pan of gently simmering water (make sure the base of the bowl does not touch the water).

3   Fold all the remaining ingredients into the melted butter and chocolate.

4   Pour the mixture into the lined tin and bake for 45–50 minutes until the mixture still has a slight wobble – it should be a little gooey in the middle. If you prefer it more cooked, then leave it in the oven a little longer.

5   Leave to cool in the tin, then slice into portions. Serve cold or warmed up, with vanilla ice cream.

Peaches are a summer delight and this dessert really celebrates this beautiful fruit. The recipe will work well with other fruit, but this version is a Galetti favourite. If you don't have peaches to hand, try it with strawberries, really soft, ripe pears or rhubarb that's been roasted with sugar until tender.

PEACHIE MESS

SERVES 4-6

FOR THE PEACH ICE CREAM

300g peaches (skinned and pitted), frozen

150g crème fraîche

1 tablespoon golden syrup

½ teaspoon vanilla bean paste

FOR THE WHIPPED CREAM

200g whipping cream

1 tablespoon icing sugar

½ teaspoon vanilla bean paste

FOR THE ROASTED PEACHES

2 tablespoons caster sugar

4 ripe peaches, stoned and quartered

50g unsalted butter

TO FINISH

½ batch of Meringue (see page 148)

2 tablespoons chopped salted pistachio nuts

1 For the peach ice cream, place the frozen peaches in a blender and blitz until smooth. Mix in the remaining ingredients, then keep in the freezer until needed.

2 For the whipped cream, whisk the ingredients together with an electric hand whisk to stiff peaks, then chill.

3 For the roasted peaches, heat a large frying pan over a medium heat and sprinkle the sugar evenly over the base. When the sugar starts to caramelize, add the peaches, then the butter. Cook the peaches for about 4 minutes until nicely caramelized, then leave to cool to room temperature.

4 Break up the meringue in serving bowls and top with the roasted peaches. Add some of the whipped cream and the peach ice cream, then scatter with the chopped pistachios.

Sharing good food with your children is the purest form of love. I'll never forget the time my father came running out as I was leaving his house holding a banana on a fork, to keep my hunger at bay – it still makes me laugh today! This banana cake recipe has been altered and adapted over the years and my daughter Anais has been making it with me since she was about eight years old. Nowadays she doesn't need my help – well, maybe with the cleaning up afterwards. And the eating, of course.

ANAIS'S BANANA LOAF CAKE

SERVES 6–8

100g unsalted butter, softened

3 tablespoons honey, plus extra to serve

2 eggs

50ml milk

1 teaspoon vanilla bean paste

1 teaspoon baking powder

225g self-raising flour

½ teaspoon ground cinnamon

½ teaspoon ground nutmeg

3 ripe bananas, well mashed

TO SERVE

2 bananas, sliced

200g Greek yogurt

50g walnuts

1 Preheat the oven to 160°C fan, Gas Mark 4. Butter a 22 x 11cm loaf tin and line it with nonstick baking paper.

2 Whisk the soft butter with the honey using an electric hand whisk for 2 minutes until light and airy.

3 Whisk in the eggs, milk and vanilla bean paste, then whisk in the baking powder, one-third of the flour and all the spices.

4 Fold through the remaining flour by hand, then stir in the mashed bananas.

5 Pour the mixture into the prepared tin and bake for 1 hour, or until a skewer inserted into the centre comes out clean.

6 Leave the cake to rest in the tin for 5 minutes before turning out onto a wire rack.

7 Serve with the sliced bananas and dollops of the yogurt, sprinkled with the walnuts and drizzled with a little honey.

One of my happiest memories is coming home to Mum when she had baked her chocolate cookies, especially as she would be at work most evenings, so it was a double treat to have her home. My cousins used to love her cookies so much that they called her Auntie Cookie! I now make these for my daughter and unfortunately they don't last long in our household.

DOUBLE CHOCOLATE CHIP COOKIES

MAKES 22

125g soft unsalted butter

150g light muscovado sugar

250g plain flour

4g (scant teaspoon) baking powder

8g cocoa powder

1 egg

90g dark chocolate chips

90g milk chocolate chips

1   Preheat the oven to 180°C fan, Gas Mark 6. Line a large baking tray with nonstick baking paper.

2   Cream the butter and sugar until fluffy.

3   Sift in the flour, baking powder and cocoa powder, then add the egg and mix well. Stir in the chocolate chips.

4   Divide the dough into 22 equal-sized pieces and roll into balls. At this stage you can freeze the dough to bake another day.

5   Place the balls on the prepared tray, spaced 3cm apart, and gently press each to flatten.

6   Bake for 10 minutes or until golden.

7   Cool on a wire rack and store in an airtight container for up to 3 days.

When we have fruit that is starting to look a little worse for wear, I drop it into a container for the freezer. It can be anything, such as bananas, apples (peeled and cored first) or berries, and it doesn't matter if they are mixed together. My daughter regularly uses this frozen fruit mix to blend herself a quickie ice cream on a hot day. The yogurt makes it a creamier mix, but it works just as well with milk – just don't add too much or it will turn into a smoothie!

QUICKIE ICE CREAM

SERVES 4–6

210g frozen mixed berries
210g frozen mango pieces
200g natural yogurt, or 200ml milk

1   Place all the ingredients in a blender and blitz until smooth. Serve immediately.

Family is my foundation. They are my sounding block. They keep me grounded, whole and loved. They are the ones who love me unconditionally, through the good and the bad, and are those who truly know me.

I come from the background of an enormous Pacific Island family: we are more like a community. So on leaving and moving to the UK back in 1999, it took me a few years to truly settle and call London my home. It was only made easier when I found a network of friends who to this day I call my UK family – my nearest and dearest friends who mean the most to me.

Sometimes we don't get to spend as much time together as we would like, but when we do, time rolls back, the music is on, the table is struggling from the weight of food, wine is flowing, conversation and laughter are deafening... This is when I'm at my happiest, being with my loved ones and creating beautiful memories around the table, enjoying great food and company.

FAMILY GET-TOGETHERS

CONTENTS

Mackerel is such a tasty and affordable fish and I enjoy it in many forms, both at home and at my restaurant. In this recipe it's simply coated in mustard and flour and cooked in oil. A refreshing pickled cucumber salad completes the dish.

MACKEREL WITH PICKLED CUCUMBER SALAD

SERVES 4–6

6 large mackerel fillets, about 110g each

1 tablespoon Dijon mustard

200g plain flour

250ml rapeseed oil

2 lemons, cut into wedges

salt and pepper

FOR THE PICKLED CUCUMBER SALAD

1 cucumber, halved lengthways, seeds scraped out with a spoon, finely sliced

2 celery sticks, peeled and finely sliced

100ml white balsamic vinegar

2 Little Gem lettuces, leaves separated and torn

2 tablespoons chopped tarragon leaves

2 tablespoons extra virgin olive oil

2 tablespoons capers

1 For the pickled cucumber salad, put the cucumber and celery in a bowl, add the vinegar and leave to pickle for 20 minutes. Then drain the vegetables, reserving the pickling vinegar.

2 Place the lettuce in a bowl and toss through the pickled veg. Add the tarragon to the reserved vinegar. Stir through the extra virgin olive oil. Season with a little salt and pepper and drizzle over the salad leaves.

3 Make sure the fish fillets have no pin bones – feel down the centre of each fillet for the tips of the bones and pluck out any you find with tweezers.

4 Brush the fillets with the mustard. Season the flour with a little salt and pepper and lightly coat the fish pieces with it.

5 Heat a large frying pan with the rapeseed oil over a medium-high heat. Place 3–4 fish pieces in the pan skin-side down and gently fry for 1 minute, then flip and fry for 30 seconds. Drain on kitchen paper. Repeat with the remaining fillets.

6 Increase the heat a little and quickly fry the capers until crispy, then drain on kitchen paper. Sprinkle over the salad. Serve with the mackerel and the lemon wedges.

My husband David loves learning to cook, and since I first introduced him to curing fish it has become one of his favourite things to make. Our family is always impressed to know that it is David who has made this and not me!

DAVID'S LAGER & CITRUS CURED SALMON

SERVES 4-6

1 tablespoon fennel seeds

1 tablespoon cumin seeds

1 tablespoon coriander seeds

150g demerara sugar

340g rock salt

grated zest and juice of 2 unwaxed limes

grated zest and juice of 1 unwaxed orange

grated zest of 1 unwaxed lemon

200ml lager

1 side of salmon, about 1kg, skin-on, scaled and pin boned

lemon wedges, to serve

1 Crush the spices with a pestle and mortar. Place in a bowl and mix with the sugar, rock salt, citrus zests and juice.

2 Using a sharp knife, make 5 slits on the skin of the salmon. Place in a tray, pour over the lager, then coat with the spice and citrus mix.

3 Lay a sheet of nonstick baking paper over the fish. Place another tray on top, transfer to the refrigerator and weight it down with cartons of juice or milk. Leave to marinate for 2–3 hours.

4 Remove the fish from the refrigerator, wipe off the spice and citrus salt mix with a clean damp cloth and pat the salmon dry. Slice and serve with lemon wedges.

Prawns are always a popular option with my family, especially my daughter Anais. Sumac has a wonderful citrus flavour and works well in both meat and fish dishes. This recipe says to marinate the prawns for 20 minutes, but I find the longer the marinating time, the better the dish tastes.

PRAWNS & SUMAC IN SPAGHETTI

SERVES 4-6

20 uncooked shell-on king prawns

1 tablespoon sumac

2 garlic cloves, grated

1 tablespoon thyme leaves

olive oil

2 handfuls of spaghetti

120g pancetta, chopped

240g cream cheese

2 tablespoons chopped chives

salt and pepper

1 Remove the heads from the prawns and set them aside. Place the prawns in a bowl and mix through the sumac, garlic, thyme leaves and 2 tablespoons olive oil. Cover, and set aside for at least 20 minutes to marinate.

2 Meanwhile, place the prawn heads in a saucepan, add just enough water to cover and bring to the boil. Simmer for 5 minutes, then strain and reserve about 250ml of the stock.

3 Cook the pasta in a large pan of salted boiling water according to the packet instructions.

4 While the pasta is cooking, heat a large nonstick pan over a medium heat. Drizzle in a little olive oil and fry the pancetta until golden brown. Remove the pancetta and set aside.

5 Return the pan to the heat and cook the prawns for 2–3 minutes. Return the pancetta to the pan, then stir in the cream cheese and half the reserved stock.

6 Drain the pasta, add to the pan and toss through gently. Add more stock if needed.

7 Take off the heat, scatter over the chives and serve with a few twists of black pepper.

We love to grow a mixture of tomatoes and enjoy picking them as they ripen – having them in the garden was the best way to get my daughter to eat them when she was younger. You can use any tomatoes in this recipe, and marinating them for a little longer if you have the time will really get the flavours developing with the spices and allow their natural juices to flow, which is key once the croutons have been added.

TOMATOES IN SUMMER

SERVES 4–6

2 punnets of ripe red cherry tomatoes, about 250g in total, halved

2 punnets of ripe yellow cherry tomatoes, about 250g in total, halved

½ teaspoon coriander seeds

½ teaspoon cumin seeds

½ teaspoon celery salt

3 garlic cloves, 2 grated, 1 peeled but left whole

2 tablespoons lemon thyme leaves

200g podded broad beans

350g sourdough bread slices

olive oil

100g green olives, pitted

1 small bunch of basil leaves

salt and pepper

1 Place all the tomatoes in a bowl.

2 Heat a small frying pan over a medium-high heat, add the spice seeds and toast until they smell aromatic. Crush with a pestle and mortar, then add to the tomatoes.

3 Add the celery salt, grated garlic and the lemon thyme leaves and mix through. Cover and set aside at room temperature for at least 20 minutes to marinate.

4 Meanwhile, blanch the broad beans in a pan of boiling water for 2–3 minutes, then drain and when cool enough to handle remove the skins.

5 Preheat the oven to 180°C fan, Gas Mark 6.

6 Rub the sourdough all over with the remaining garlic clove. Tear it into bite-sized pieces, place on a baking tray and drizzle with a little olive oil. Bake for a few minutes until crispy. Leave to cool, then fold through the tomatoes.

7 Add the broad beans and olives, season with salt and pepper and then sprinkle over the basil leaves.

This is a kind of warm salad – I love it so much I could eat it every day. In the summer it's perfect when you cook the carrots on the barbecue and then mix them through the rest of the salad. Sometimes I like to add chicory (Belgian endive), as the extra bitterness works so well with the sweetness of the carrots. If you'd like to try it this way, cut the chicory in half lengthways (or quarter them if they're large ones) and toss with the other ingredients before you serve.

CUMIN, ORANGE & COCONUT ROASTED CARROTS

SERVES 4–6

4 bunches of baby carrots, about 200g in total, washed and green tops trimmed

1 tablespoon cumin seeds

grated zest and juice of 1 unwaxed orange

4 shallots, halved

4 garlic cloves, peeled but left whole

1 tablespoon melted coconut oil

2 tablespoons coconut flakes

½ lemon, for squeezing

2 tablespoons extra virgin olive oil

2 tablespoons flat leaf parsley leaves

1 tablespoon tarragon leaves

2 tablespoons cashew nuts, chopped

salt and pepper

1 Preheat the oven to 190°C fan, Gas Mark 6½.

2 Put the carrots in a roasting tray and season with the cumin, orange zest and half the orange juice. Add the shallots cut sides down and the garlic cloves, then drizzle with the coconut oil.

3 Cover the tray with foil and roast for about 10 minutes until tender.

4 Remove the foil and add the coconut flakes, then return to the oven and roast uncovered for a further 2–3 minutes.

5 Leave until cool enough to handle, then separate the shallots into petals.

6 Mash the roasted garlic cloves in a small bowl. Add a few drops of lemon juice, the remaining orange juice and the extra virgin olive oil, and season to taste with salt and pepper.

7 Pour over the warm carrots and toss through the herbs and shallot petals. Sprinkle over the chopped cashews to finish.

This is a great one for placing in the middle of the table and letting your guests tear away at it. I use sourdough, but really any loaf will work here. The pesto can be made in a large quantity and stored in a sterilized airtight jar (see page 17) in the fridge for up to 3 weeks. Any leftover can be added to pasta or served with cooked meat or fish.

SUN-DRIED TOMATO PESTO & MOZZARELLA LOAF

SERVES 4-6

1 medium sourdough loaf

olive oil

230g Sun-Dried Tomato Pesto (see below)

1 small bunch of basil, leaves roughly chopped

400g mozzarella cheese, torn

5 anchovy fillets, rinsed and patted dry, then cut into small pieces

salt and pepper

FOR THE SUN-DRIED TOMATO PESTO (MAKES ABOUT 400G)

110g sun-dried tomatoes

1 garlic clove, grated

80g pine nuts

1 small bunch of basil

110g Parmesan cheese, grated

110ml olive oil

1   For the pesto, place the sun-dried tomatoes with the garlic in a blender and pulse until finely chopped. Add the pine nuts and pulse until chopped, making sure not to blend the mixture to a fine paste.

2   Add the basil and Parmesan and again pulse to blend through. Blend in the olive oil and then correct the seasoning with salt and pepper to taste.

3   Cut a few slices into the loaf about 3.5cm thick but not all the way through – you want the base of the loaf to hold the slices in place. Turn the loaf and cut across the slices in the same way, so that it looks like a hedgehog.

4   Spread open the loaf and drizzle the inside liberally with olive oil, then spread the pesto through the insides.

5   Place the basil inside the loaf, then wedge the mozzarella pieces inside. Finally, add the anchovy pieces. Drizzle with a little more olive oil, then set aside for at least 20 minutes before baking.

6   Preheat the oven to 180°C fan, Gas Mark 6.

7   Place the loaf on a baking tray and cover with foil. Bake for 12 minutes, then remove the foil and bake for a further 2–3 minutes. Serve immediately.

Chimichurri and grilled meat is a match made in heaven – then
add a burnt butter mash and you're guaranteed to have a very
happy family gathering! I like to keep the seeds in the chillies
for extra heat.

STEAK, CHIMICHURRI & BURNT BUTTER MASH

SERVES 6

½ teaspoon smoked paprika

6 onglet or hanger steaks, about 220g each

olive oil

salt and pepper

FOR THE CHIMICHURRI

50g flat leaf parsley leaves

3 garlic cloves, peeled

1 red chilli, deseeded (or not, if you prefer)

grated zest and juice of 1 unwaxed lemon

1 tablespoon fresh oregano leaves

120ml extra virgin olive oil

FOR THE BURNT BUTTER MASH

4 King Edwards or other floury potatoes, peeled and roughly chopped

120ml double cream

100ml milk

160g unsalted butter

1 For the chimichurri, finely mince the parsley, garlic and chilli together. Place in a serving dish, add the remaining ingredients and whisk together, then season to taste with salt and pepper.

2 For the mash, cook the potatoes in a large pan of boiling salted water for 15 minutes or until cooked, then drain well.

3 While the potatoes are cooking, rub the smoked paprika and some salt and pepper into the steaks and leave to sit for 20 minutes at room temperature.

4 Preheat a barbecue, or a griddle pan, over a high heat.

5 Drizzle some olive oil over the steaks and cook on the hot barbecue or griddle pan – they should take about 2 minutes on each side for medium-rare, depending on how hot the barbecue is. Leave to rest for 5 minutes.

6 While the steaks are cooking and resting, warm the cream and milk for the mash in a saucepan.

7 Mash the potatoes, using a potato ricer if you have one.

8 Place the butter in the pan the potatoes were cooked in and cook to a nutty brown. Add the mash and stir. Gradually beat in the warm cream mixture, allowing each addition to absorb well before the next. Season to taste with salt and pepper.

9 Carve the steaks, place on a platter with the chimichurri and serve with the mash.

There's something about spicy chicken wings – everyone just devours them. And if there's ever a group of people to share them with, when you are free to eat with your hands and be messy, it's definitely got to be friends and family! The sheer pleasure of these wings is getting stuck in – and the more the merrier!

HOT SESAME CHICKEN WINGS

MAKES 24

150g cornflour

about 150ml sparkling water

300ml rapeseed oil

24 large chicken wings

400g sriracha sauce

2 garlic cloves, finely grated

2 tablespoons chilli paste, such as gochujang

1 teaspoon soy sauce

2 tablespoons honey

1 tablespoon sesame seeds

2 spring onions, finely sliced

salt and pepper

1   Place the cornflour in a bowl and make a well in the centre. Gradually pour in enough of the sparkling water while whisking until you have a batter thick enough to coat the chicken wings.

2   Heat the rapeseed oil in a deep saucepan to 180°C (make sure the pan is no more than one-third full with oil).

3   Dry the wings on kitchen paper, then season with a little salt and pepper and coat in the batter, wiping off any excess on the side of the bowl.

4   Fry 3–4 wings at a time for just a few minutes, turning often until golden brown and cooked through. Drain on kitchen paper.

5   While the wings are frying, heat the sriracha, garlic, chilli paste, soy and honey in a saucepan and bring to the boil, stirring.

6   Place the fried wings in a bowl and pour over the hot sauce, then gently mix with the sesame seeds to coat the wings. Sprinkle the spring onions over the top and serve immediately.

This lamb dish releases the aroma of spices into the kitchen while it cooks, and never fails to whet the appetite. I know it's a winner as my Mum-in-law, who doesn't usually eat lamb, comes back for seconds. If you aren't a Marmite fan, feel free to omit it – but you don't know what you're missing!

SPICE-RUBBED ROAST LAMB

SERVES 4-6

1 lamb shoulder, about 1.5kg

4 garlic cloves, peeled

1 teaspoon cumin seeds

1 teaspoon coriander seeds

½ teaspoon ground cinnamon

2 tablespoons sea salt flakes

2 tablespoons soft light brown sugar

leaves from 2 rosemary sprigs, chopped

1 tablespoon tomato purée

1 tablespoon Marmite

4 ripe tomatoes, chopped

300ml lamb stock

60g unsalted butter, optional

3 handfuls of spinach

1. Preheat the oven to 170°C fan, Gas Mark 5.

2. Trim the lamb of any excess fat. Make incisions at intervals in the lamb deep enough to hold the garlic cloves and then push them in.

3. Mix the spices, sea salt, sugar and rosemary together in a bowl.

4. Place the lamb in a large roasting tin and rub the spice mix into the meat.

5. Cover with foil and roast for 55 minutes. Turn the shoulder over and roast for a further 55 minutes. Remove the shoulder from the tin and keep warm.

6. Add the tomato purée to the juices in the tin and cook over a medium heat for 1 minute. Add the Marmite, tomatoes and lamb stock and bring to the boil, then reduce the heat to a simmer and cook for 5 minutes.

7. Add the butter (if using) and stir in the spinach to wilt. Correct the seasoning with salt and pepper to taste.

8. Shred the lamb and serve over the tomato and spinach.

Believe it or not, corned beef is quite a big thing within the Samoan community. Apparently, the local name for it was derived from the first canned product introduced to Samoa – pea soup. Because in the Samoan language words can't end with a consonant, they tagged an 'o' on to the end, and for some reason the word *pisupo* has come to mean corned beef. I have fond memories as a child of having it added to sautéed onions and cabbage. I rarely eat it nowadays, but every time my family visit, I am guaranteed to receive at least four to six cans of the Samoan *pisupo*.

CORNED BEEF HASHCAKES WITH PICCALILLI

MAKES 12

3 large King Edwards or other floury potatoes, washed and dried

300g canned corned beef

3 spring onions, finely sliced

plain flour

2 eggs

butter

pepper

FOR THE PICCALILLI (MAKES ABOUT 750G)

250g cauliflower florets

1 carrot, peeled and cut into small dice

1 courgette, cut into small dice

150g baby onions, quartered

150g French beans, trimmed and cut into small batons

150g rock salt

1 tablespoon mustard powder

1 tablespoon yellow mustard seeds

150g sugar

1 tablespoon thyme leaves

1 bay leaf

500ml white wine vinegar

1 tablespoon water

2 tablespoons cornflour

1 teaspoon ground turmeric

For method, see overleaf

1   Prepare the piccalilli 1–2 weeks ahead: Place the prepared vegetables in a large bowl, sprinkling layers of the rock salt in between. Pour over enough water to cover and leave to soak overnight.

2   Next day, drain and rinse the vegetables under cold water.

3   Place the mustard powder and seeds, sugar, herbs and 200ml of the vinegar in a large saucepan and heat until the sugar has dissolved.

4   Add the vegetables and bring to the boil, then reduce the heat to a simmer and cook for 10–15 minutes.

5   Mix the remaining vinegar and the 1 tablespoon of water with the cornflour and turmeric. Stir into the vegetables and return to the boil, then simmer gently until nice and thick.

6   Transfer to warm, sterilized airtight jars (see page 17) and store for 1–2 weeks before opening. Once open, keep refrigerated and use within a month.

7   To make the hashcakes, preheat the oven to 180°C fan, Gas Mark 6.

8   Place the potatoes directly on the oven shelf and bake for 45 minutes–1 hour or until cooked through. Leave until cool enough to handle, then cut in half lengthways, scoop the flesh out into a large bowl and mash while still a little warm.

9   Break up the corned beef and mix through. Add the spring onions with 1 tablespoon flour, season with pepper and mix in the eggs until well combined.

10 Divide the potato mixture into 6–8 equal amounts and form into firm balls, then gently flatten to make patties. Place on a plate and keep chilled until needed.

11 When ready to cook, preheat the oven to 180°C fan, Gas Mark 6.

12 Lightly dust the hashcakes in flour and gently fry in a little butter in a frying pan for a few minutes until golden on both sides. Transfer the hashcakes to a baking tray and cook in the oven for 3–5 minutes to completely heat through. Serve with the piccalilli.

Cauliflower is such a simple vegetable and can be so delicious. Here it is a star on its own and, cooked this way, it makes a regular appearance in my kitchen both at home and in my restaurant. We have it almost once a week – it's perfect as a main or a side. Cauliflower takes well to a host of other spices, so, if you'd like a change once you've tried this version, try substituting smoked paprika for the turmeric and garam masala for another great way to enjoy it.

WHOLE BAKED CAULIFLOWER

SERVES 4-6

½ teaspoon ground turmeric

½ teaspoon garam masala

60ml extra virgin olive oil

2 pinches of salt

I large cauliflower, large outer leaves removed

Rocket Pesto (see page 170–1), to serve

1 Preheat the oven to 190°C fan, Gas Mark 6½.

2 Mix the turmeric, garam masala, extra virgin olive oil and salt together in a bowl.

3 Place the cauliflower in a roasting tray and brush all over with the spice and oil mixture.

4 Cover the tray with foil and bake for 1¼ hours.

5 Leave to rest, covered with the foil, for 15 minutes before carving. Serve with the rocket pesto.

I've been very lucky to have worked with so many Italian chefs who have taught me how to make a decent pizza at home. This is my favourite, but go ahead and swap these ingredients for your own and have fun choosing toppings with your family and friends. The only rule in my house is: no pineapple!

AUBERGINE & ANCHOVY PIZZA

MAKES 4 MEDIUM OR 6 SMALL PIZZAS

FOR THE PIZZA DOUGH

7g sachet fast-action dried yeast, or 10g fresh yeast, crumbled

350ml warm water

500g strong white flour, plus extra for dusting

10g salt

semolina, for dusting

FOR THE TOMATO SAUCE

1 onion, sliced

4 garlic cloves, chopped

olive oil

2 tablespoons tomato purée

400g can chopped tomatoes

1 teaspoon dried oregano

salt and pepper

FOR THE TOPPING

2 large aubergines, cut into 5mm-thick rounds

olive oil

150g Cheddar cheese, grated

20 anchovy fillets (if they are very salty, lightly rinse and pat dry)

150g feta cheese

For method, see overleaf

1 Stir the yeast into 100ml of the warm water and leave for 10 minutes to activate.

2 Mix the flour and salt together in a bowl and make a well in the centre. Pour in the yeast mixture and the remaining warm water and gradually mix in to form a dough.

3 Knead the dough on a lightly floured work surface for about 10 minutes until smooth and elastic. Return to the bowl, cover and leave to rest at room temperature for 20 minutes or in the refrigerator overnight.

4 If the dough has risen, knead it lightly – the longer you leave it, the more it will rise.

5 For the tomato sauce, sweat the onion and garlic in a little olive oil in a pan over a medium heat until translucent.

6 Add the tomato purée and cook for 2 minutes. Add the chopped tomatoes and oregano, season to taste with salt and pepper and simmer for about 20 minutes until you have a thick sauce, then leave to cool.

7 Meanwhile, for the topping, preheat the oven to 180°C fan, Gas Mark 6.

8 Place the aubergine slices on a baking tray, brush or drizzle with a little olive oil and roast for 20 minutes until soft. Set aside but leave the oven on.

9 Divide the dough into 4 and press out into rounds of your desired thickness – for me, the thinner the better!

10 Transfer the rounds to 2 large baking trays dusted with semolina and spread the with the tomato sauce. Scatter over half the Cheddar.

11 Add the aubergine and sprinkle the anchovies around. Crumble the feta over the top and sprinkle over the remaining Cheddar.

12 Cover and leave to prove for 15 minutes at room temperature. Meanwhile, increase the oven temperature to 200°C fan, Gas Mark 7.

13 Bake the pizzas for about 20 minutes until golden and bubbling.

This is one of my go-to entertaining recipes. The first time
I made it, I didn't have enough individual ovenproof bowls,
so I decided to make one for everyone to share by using a large
flan dish instead. The surprise on their faces when they saw it
made it all the more worthwhile, so that's how I serve it all the
time now. It's a rare thing to have leftovers, but a certain friend
of ours has been known to take the whole dish home.

MONSTER RHUBARB CRÈME BRÛLÉE

SERVES 6–8

4 large rhubarb stalks, about 800g, trimmed
and roughly chopped

grated zest and juice of 1 unwaxed orange

100g demerara sugar

550ml double cream

110ml milk

120g caster sugar, plus extra for the topping

7 large egg yolks

1 Place the rhubarb in a small saucepan with the orange zest and juice and demerara sugar. Stew over a gentle heat for about 5 minutes to a thick compote consistency. Leave to cool and keep chilled until needed.

2 Bring the cream and milk to the boil in a saucepan.

3 Meanwhile, whisk the caster sugar and egg yolks together in a large bowl just until mixed. Pour the hot cream mixture into the bowl with the eggs while whisking continuously.

4 Return the mixture to the pan and cook over a medium-low heat, stirring continuously, until thick enough to coat the back of a spoon – just before the custard comes to the boil, or when it reaches 82°C on a thermometer. Pass through a fine sieve into a clean bowl.

5 Preheat the oven to 110°C fan, Gas Mark ¾.

6 Drain the chilled rhubarb compote of excess juice (but don't throw it away – it's delicious as a topping for yogurt) and place the compote in a 24cm diameter flan dish. Smooth it out to cover the base. Pour the custard over the rhubarb.

7 Bake for 55 minutes or until just beginning to firm. Leave at room temperature to cool and set.

8 To serve, sprinkle a layer of caster sugar over the top and use a blowtorch to glaze to a golden brown colour. Allow to cool before serving.

My daughter Anais has been cooking with me since she was able to walk. I love that the praise she has had for her shortbreads has encouraged her to make them more often than just for family gatherings. And always the proud mum, I get a buzz watching her face light up when other people rave about how tasty they are. I want to say 'She gets it from her mama,' but apparently that's not cool...

ANAIS'S GINGER & LIME SHORTBREAD

MAKES 12

250g plain flour

¼ teaspoon ground ginger

75g caster sugar, plus extra for dusting

grated zest of 2 unwaxed limes, plus extra for decorating

160g unsalted butter, cubed

1 Preheat the oven to 160°C fan, Gas Mark 4.

2 Sift the flour and ginger together into a bowl. Stir in the sugar and lime zest.

3 Rub in the butter until the mixture comes together into a dough.

4 Place the dough on a baking tray and either press or roll out into a rectangle about 1.5cm thick.

5 Using a knife, score into fingers, then bake for 30–35 minutes or until pale golden.

6 Dust with grated lime zest and caster sugar, then leave to cool on the tray before cutting into fingers. Store in an airtight container for up to 3 days.

A baked Alaska is great for entertaining. You can literally make one up in advance with the meringue on top and then freeze it for 2–3 days, so all you need to do is take it out of the freezer for a few minutes, then put it straight into the oven. If you can't get your hands on white chocolate ice cream, a good vanilla will do the trick – or use whatever flavour you have in the freezer.

LEMON & WHITE CHOCOLATE BAKED ALASKA

SERVES 10–12

FOR THE SPONGE
unsalted butter, for greasing

25g honey

2 teaspoons water

2 medium eggs (100g in total)

60g caster sugar

60g plain flour, sifted, plus extra for dusting

FOR THE LEMON CURD
5 large egg yolks (100g in total)

1 large egg (50g)

90ml lemon juice

40g caster sugar

60g cold unsalted butter, cubed

FOR THE ITALIAN MERINGUE
170g caster sugar

4 tablespoons water

3 large egg whites (90g in total)

450g white chocolate ice cream, slightly softened

1   For the sponge, preheat the oven to 160°C fan, Gas Mark 4. Grease and line a 20cm diameter cake tin with nonstick baking paper.

2   Warm the honey and the water in a small saucepan.

3   Whisk the eggs and sugar together using an electric hand whisk until the mixture leaves a ribbon-like trail. Whisk in the honey solution. Add the flour and fold in by hand.

4   Pour the mixture into the prepared tin and bake for about 10 minutes or until a light golden colour and the sponge bounces back when lightly pressed. Turn out on to a wire rack to cool.

5   Clean the cake tin and line it with clingfilm.

6   To make the lemon curd, place the egg yolks and whole egg, lemon juice and sugar in a large saucepan over a medium-low heat and whisk until you have a very thick curd. Leave to cool to room temperature, then gradually beat in the cubed butter.

7   Press the slightly softened ice cream into the base of the lined cake tin, then spread the curd on top. Put the sponge disk on top of the curd, then place in the freezer for 1 hour to set.

8   Once set, place a flat ovenproof plate on top of the sponge and invert the tin so the sponge is on the base.

9   For the meringue, heat the sugar and the water in a saucepan until the sugar has dissolved, then increase the heat and simmer until the sugar syrup is at 120°C – you will need to use a sugar thermometer.

10 At the same time, whisk the egg whites to stiff peaks using an electric hand whisk or stand mixer.

11 Set aside the hot sugar syrup for 30 seconds, then pour it in a long, steady stream on to the egg whites while whisking continuously. Continue whisking until the meringue has cooled.

12 Meanwhile, preheat the oven to 180°C fan, Gas Mark 6.

13 Spread or pipe the meringue to cover the ice cream, then bake for 3–4 minutes or until lightly brown. Serve immediately.

What's great about this tart is that you can make everything
a day or two beforehand and assemble it when it's needed.
The pistachio cream can be kept in the fridge for 3–4 days –
just whip it up for 2 minutes if it has set when you're ready
to use it. And it's also an easy recipe to swap in different fruits,
so use the best of the season, or whatever you have to hand.

RASPBERRY & PISTACHIO TART

SERVES 4–6

220g thick-set raspberry jam

400g raspberries

25g chopped pistachio nuts

small bunch of mint

FOR THE PASTRY

240g soft unsalted butter

120g caster sugar

1 egg

350g plain flour, plus extra for dusting

1–2 tablespoons water

FOR THE PISTACHIO CREAM

190ml milk

seeds scraped from 1 vanilla pod

3 large egg yolks (60g in total)

40g caster sugar

20g cornflour

20g plain flour

40g pistachio paste (available online)

60g cold unsalted butter, cubed

100g double cream, whipped

1   For the pastry, beat the butter and sugar together in a bowl until fully creamed, then beat in the egg. Fold in the flour without overmixing. Add the water as needed to bring the mixture together into a dough. Wrap and chill for 30 minutes.

2   Preheat the oven to 180°C fan, Gas Mark 6.

3   Roll out the pastry on a lightly floured work surface, or between 2 sheets of greaseproof paper, and use to line a 22cm diameter 2cm deep fluted tart tin.

4   Line the pastry with nonstick baking paper and fill with uncooked rice or baking beans, then blind bake for 10 minutes. Remove the paper and rice, or beans, and bake for a further 6 minutes or until golden, then leave to cool.

5   For the pistachio cream, heat the milk with the vanilla seeds in a saucepan.

6   Whisk the egg yolks, sugar and flours together in a bowl. Pour the hot milk over the egg mixture while whisking continuously until very thick. Return to the pan and cook over a medium-low heat, whisking continuously, until thick and starting to boil.

7   Take the pan off the heat and whisk in the pistachio paste, then the cold butter. Leave to cool in the refrigerator, then fold in the whipped cream.

8   Spread the jam in an even layer over the base of the cooked tart case. Pipe or spread the pistachio cream on top, then chill for a minimum of 2 hours.

9   Decorate with the raspberries, pistachios and mint leaves, and keep chilled before serving.

Pratish is one of my dearest friends, and he has a very sweet tooth. It's just as well he happens to be a dentist or we'd all be in trouble. Every time I ask him what dessert he wants, he'll normally say, 'Anything would be lovely, but I do love Black Forest cake,' so I thought I'd adapt a cheesecake to suit. He wasn't best pleased when I once sent this recipe to his husband Craig – Prat arrived home to find he not only had to help Craig finish making it, but he had to clean up a disaster of a mess in the kitchen too.

BLACK FOREST CHEESECAKE FOR PRAT

SERVES 10–12
(OR JUST PRAT ON HIS OWN)

140g fresh cherries, pitted

500g full-fat cream cheese

250g double cream

80g icing sugar

100g dark chocolate (70% cocoa), melted, plus large shavings to decorate

1 tablespoon kirsch

FOR THE BISCUIT BASE

250g digestive biscuits

100g unsalted butter, melted

1 teaspoon cocoa powder

1 tablespoon soft light brown sugar

1 For the biscuit base, place all the ingredients in a food processor and pulse to a crumb. Press into a 20cm springform cake tin and halfway up the sides, then chill to set.

2 Chop half the cherries and reserve the rest whole for decorating.

3 Whisk the cream cheese, cream and icing sugar together in a bowl until you have a thick mixture, then fold through the melted chocolate, chopped cherries and kirsch.

4 Pour the cream cheese mixture over the biscuit base and refrigerate to set, ideally overnight.

5 Remove from the cake tin and top with large shavings of dark chocolate and the reserved whole cherries.

I remember Mum making a steamed pudding, or *puligi* in Samoan, served with lashings of ice cream, which is still how I love it. Here, I've adapted her recipe to include treacle and maple syrup, which I absolutely love as well. My dear friend Shawn is a dab hand at puddings, so I was thrilled to have his seal of approval, too. His French husband Jerome (my husband David's bestie) eats it smothered in so much crème anglaise you can hardly see the pudding!

MAPLE & TREACLE STEAMED PUDDING FOR SHEROME (AKA SHAWN & JEROME)

SERVES 4–6, DEPENDING ON WHICH FAMILY MEMBERS

100g soft unsalted butter, plus extra for greasing

225g self-raising flour, plus extra for dusting

pinch of fine salt

1 teaspoon mixed spice

80g maple syrup

100g black treacle

½ teaspoon bicarbonate of soda

60ml milk

2 eggs

TO SERVE

100g maple syrup or treacle

pouring cream or vanilla ice cream

1 Grease a 1.2-litre pudding basin and dust with a little flour.

2 Sift the flour, salt and mixed spice together into a large bowl.

3 Warm the maple syrup, butter and treacle in a saucepan.

4 In a separate bowl, beat the bicarbonate of soda into the milk and eggs.

5 Add the maple syrup mixture and the egg and milk mixture into the flour and spices, then stir until combined. Pour into the prepared basin.

6 Grease and flour a piece of foil and use it to loosely cover the basin.

7 Place the basin in a large saucepan filled halfway with boiling water, cover and steam for 1½–2 hours, topping up the steamer with more boiling water as necessary.

8 Turn the pudding out and serve with maple syrup or treacle, cream or vanilla ice cream.

This cake actually came about while I was making a carrot cake, and just as I was about to add the carrots to the mixture, I was told that someone didn't eat carrots. So the only other veg in the fridge that I could use were courgettes. I was very close to using the beetroot, but my husband David's face said it all. (It actually works very well with beetroot – honestly!)

COURGETTE CAKE WITH WALNUTS & CRÈME CHEESE

SERVES 4–6

unsalted butter, for greasing

300g plain flour, plus extra for dusting

15g baking powder

1 teaspoon ground cinnamon

1 teaspoon ground ginger

½ teaspoon ground cloves

150g soft light brown sugar

3 eggs

¼ teaspoon salt

120g golden syrup

200ml sunflower oil

230g courgettes, grated

50g walnuts, chopped

FOR THE CRÈME CHEESE ICING

400g full-fat cream cheese

200g mascarpone

80g caster sugar

2 teaspoons vanilla bean paste

1 Preheat the oven to 170°C fan, Gas Mark 5. Grease two 22cm cake tins and dust with a little flour.

2 Sift the flour, baking powder and spices together.

3 Whisk together the brown sugar, eggs, salt and golden syrup with an electric hand whisk until pale and well-aerated. Slowly add the sunflower oil while whisking.

4 Fold in the flour mixture by hand a little at a time, then add the courgettes and most of the walnuts, reserving 10g for the top.

5 Divide the cake mixture between the prepared cake tins and bake for 30 minutes or until a skewer inserted into the centres comes out clean. Turn out on to a wire rack to cool.

6 Meanwhile, beat all the ingredients for the cream cheese icing together in a bowl. Spread one cake sponge with some of the cream cheese icing and sandwich the other cake sponge on top. Spread the top of the cake with the rest of the icing and sprinkle over the reserved walnuts to decorate.

Now, this is well and truly a childhood favourite of mine. My sister and I used to giggle hysterically whenever Dad would ask for some... 'Can you get me some of that pabalova?' Family times together are always full of so much laughter, as they should be. I tend to make this for Christmas, especially in years when I can't get back to New Zealand.

COCONUT CREAM PAVLOVA

SERVES 4-6

FOR THE MERINGUE
5 egg whites (160g)

210g caster sugar

2 teaspoons cornflour

2 teaspoons white wine vinegar

FOR THE COCONUT CREAM
150g coconut yogurt

350g double cream

2 tablespoons icing sugar

1 teaspoon vanilla bean paste

FOR THE RASPBERRY SAUCE
450g raspberries

2 tablespoons icing sugar

juice of 1 lemon

FOR THE TOPPING
1 punnet of strawberries, about 250g, sliced

2 kiwi fruit, peeled and sliced

1 punnet of blueberries, about 125g

2 tablespoons chopped pistachio nuts

2 tablespoons dried cranberries

1   Preheat the oven to 160°C fan, Gas Mark 4. Line a baking tray with nonstick baking paper.

2   For the meringue, whisk the egg whites in a large bowl to stiff peaks using an electric hand whisk, then gradually whisk in the sugar.

3   Mix the cornflour into the vinegar in a small bowl to make a slurry, then add to the egg whites and whisk through.

4   Spread the meringue on to the lined baking tray into a circle about 20cm in diameter.

5   Reduce the oven temperature to 150°C fan, Gas Mark 3½, and bake the meringue for 40–50 minutes.

6   Turn the oven off and leave the meringue inside to cool with the door slightly ajar.

7   For the coconut cream, whisk all the ingredients together in a bowl and keep chilled.

8   For the raspberry sauce, blend the ingredients together in a blender and keep chilled. If it's too thick, stir in a little water.

9   To assemble, spread the coconut cream over the cooled meringue and arrange the fruit and nuts on top. Either pour the raspberry sauce on to the pavlova or serve it on the side.

This chapter is a collection of our favourite recipes from family holidays together – in the summer and winter time. My life as a chef, running a restaurant, filming television programmes and being a mum keeps me pretty busy, and I'll often find that my calendar is completely booked up with work well into the following year. So being organized and fitting in family time is crucial, even if it's just a three-day staycation at home in south London.

Wherever we are and whatever we're celebrating, some of the best moments in the year are when we're enjoying great and fun food together with friends and family.

I hope you'll enjoy some of these recipes on one of your holidays!

HOLIDAY FAVOURITES

CONTENTS

There are so many ways to cure fish, and most recently I've started using kombucha, which works in a similar way to cider. My Mum used to make kombucha when we were kids, as she knew back then of its health benefits, and in the last few years it has become a huge trend. I would run from the kitchen when she was moving her scoby to a new home and now here I am with cupboards full of it and putting it in my cooking! I can just see her rolling her eyes and laughing at me.

KOMBUCHA & GINGER CURED MONKFISH

SERVES 4–6

500g monkfish fillet

200g rock salt

150g demerara sugar

4cm piece of fresh root ginger, peeled and grated

grated zest and juice of 2 unwaxed lemons

1 tablespoon coriander seeds, crushed

250ml kombucha

65ml olive oil

1 teaspoon honey

½ teaspoon mild curry powder

200g Greek yogurt

salt and pepper

1 small bunch of coriander, roughly chopped, to serve

1   Remove any membrane from the fish and place in a tray.

2   Mix together the salt, sugar, ginger, lemon zest, crushed coriander seeds and kombucha in a bowl. Rub liberally into the fish.

3   Lay a sheet of nonstick baking paper over the fish. Place another tray on top, transfer to the refrigerator and weight it down with cartons of milk or juice. Leave to marinate for 40 minutes.

4   Remove the fish from the refrigerator, wipe off the salt mix with a clean damp cloth and pat the fish dry. Slice the fish thinly and place on a platter.

5   To make the dressing, whisk the lemon juice with the olive oil and season with salt and pepper.

6   Whisk the honey and curry powder together, then beat in the yogurt.

7   Drizzle the fish with the dressing and the curried yogurt, sprinkle with the chopped coriander and serve.

If we're on holiday, where there are oysters Monica will go! Natural with lemon and a little fresh bread is how I love them best. If cooked, my favourite ways are how I first learned to serve them as a very young chef starting out in New Zealand – with bacon and Worcestershire sauce (Kilpatrick) or with butter, herbs and breadcrumbs (Rockefeller). I like a little bit of chilli sauce on mine at the end – Marie Sharp's is my favourite – but I tend not to add this to the cooking, as my husband and daughter find it too spicy.

OYSTERS KILPATRICK & ROCKEFELLER

SERVES 4-6

24 medium oysters, shucked
lemon wedges, to serve

FOR THE KILPATRICK
50g unsalted butter
2 tablespoons Worcestershire sauce
4 bacon rashers, any rind removed, finely chopped
2 tablespoons chopped flat leaf parsley leaves

FOR THE ROCKEFELLER
75g 1–2 day-old brioche
5g flat leaf parsley leaves
1 garlic clove, grated
handful of spinach
5g tarragon
100g unsalted butter

1   Divide the oysters in their half shells between 2 large baking trays.

2   For the oysters Kilpatrick, melt the butter with the Worcestershire sauce in a small saucepan until lightly foaming. Drizzle the butter over half the oysters and then sprinkle over the bacon.

3   Preheat the oven on the grill function.

4   For the oysters Rockefeller, place the brioche in a blender or food processor with half the parsley, the garlic and spinach. Blitz into a bright green crumb.

5   Roughly chop the remaining parsley and the tarragon.

6   Melt the butter in a small saucepan and add the chopped herbs. Drizzle the rest of the oysters with the herb butter, then sprinkle over the green breadcrumbs.

7   Place all the oysters under the hot grill until golden brown. Serve together on a platter with some lemon wedges.

When we visit New Zealand for family holidays, it's guaranteed that one of my very first stops will be to buy the fresh, green-lipped mussels and kumara (sweet potato). This dish is one of our favourite ways to enjoy mussels together – and it means even more to me, because I was first given this recipe by my Mum. If you are making the fries, make sure you prepare them first and get them in the oven before starting on the mussels.

CURRIED MUSSELS WITH SWEET POTATO FRIES

SERVES 4–6

olive oil

1 small onion, roughly chopped

1 garlic bulb, cut in half horizontally and broken up

2kg live mussels, beards removed, washed under the cold tap (discard any with damaged shells or open ones that don't close when lightly tapped)

200ml white wine

1 teaspoon ground turmeric

½ teaspoon chilli powder

½ teaspoon ground cumin

½ teaspoon ground coriander

100g Greek yogurt

garlic mayonnaise, to serve

FOR THE SWEET POTATO FRIES

4 sweet potatoes

100ml olive oil

2 rosemary sprigs, leaves picked and chopped

2 pinches of sea salt flakes

1 Preheat the oven to 190°C fan, Gas Mark 6½.

2 Peel and cut the sweet potatoes into fries. Toss with the olive oil, rosemary and sea salt flakes.

3 Spread out on a baking tray and bake for 15–20 minutes, tossing them halfway through.

4 Meanwhile, heat a large saucepan big enough to fit the mussels. Add a drizzle of olive oil and heat until very hot.

5 Add the onion and garlic to the pan and cook for 1–2 minutes. Add all the mussels and stir, then pour in the wine and cover the pan. Cook over a high heat, shaking the pan to toss the mussels, for 2 minutes.

6 Remove the lid and give a quick stir. If all the mussels haven't opened, then cover and cook for a further 2 minutes. Scoop out the mussels on to a large serving dish.

7 Add a drizzle of olive oil to a separate saucepan. Add the spices and stir for 1 minute.

8 Set a sieve over the pan and pass the mussel cooking juices into the spices. Bring to the boil, then reduce the heat to a simmer.

9 Stir in the yogurt and bring to the boil, then pour over the cooked mussels. Serve immediately with the sweet potato fries and some garlic mayonnaise.

Oh my goodness, this is a throwback to our holidays in Greece where we were so spoiled to have freshly made tapenade and flatbreads. We love making our own version at home and enjoy reminiscing about summer holidays. It's worth buying top-quality ingredients for this such as Nocellara olives, as they can make a huge difference to the end result. Making a big batch of the delicious savoury tapenade is worthwhile since it has so many uses, such as tossing it in pasta, or to flavour meat and fish dishes. We also like this with hummus on the side. The flatbreads are so easy – my daughter enjoys making up a small batch midweek as well.

OLIVE TAPENADE WITH WHOLEMEAL FLATBREADS

SERVES 4
(MAKES ABOUT 270G)

FOR THE OLIVE TAPENADE

250g pitted green olives

10g capers

3 anchovy fillets

1 garlic clove, grated or sliced

2 tablespoons chopped flat leaf parsley

1 teaspoon thyme leaves

½ teaspoon white wine vinegar

2 tablespoons extra virgin olive oil, plus extra for storing

FOR THE FLATBREADS

400g wholemeal self-raising flour, plus extra for dusting

6g baking powder

380g Greek yogurt

1   For the tapenade, place all the ingredients in a blender and pulse to a nice chopped texture. Don't leave the machine running, otherwise the mixture will turn into a paste. If I'm storing the tapenade in the refrigerator, I transfer it to a sterilized airtight jar (see page 17) and drizzle a little extra olive oil on top, as it stops the tapenade from oxidizing and it will keep for longer, up to 2–3 weeks.

2   For the flatbreads, mix the ingredients together in a large bowl until the mixture comes together into a firm dough. Divide the dough into 8–10 equal amounts and shape into balls. Press each ball flat on a lightly floured work surface, then roll out to a round about 5mm thick.

3   Heat a nonstick frying pan over a medium heat.

4   Cook one flatbread at a time until nice and golden on both sides and lightly puffed. Serve warm with the tapenade.

This recipe can be made without the squash and kept plain – this version came about when we had some leftover roast butternut that made its way into the hummus. The garlic cloves are gently cooked in olive oil until they are soft and sweet – I like making extra and having them on hand to use in salads and a quick aioli. Serve this with flatbreads (see recipe opposite), pickles and cooked meats.

BUTTERNUT SQUASH HUMMUS

SERVES 4–6

½ butternut squash, peeled, deseeded and cubed

olive oil

200ml water

1 tablespoon thyme leaves

4 saffron threads (optional)

400g can chickpeas, drained

120g tahini

4 Confit Garlic Cloves (see below)

½ teaspoon chilli powder

50ml extra virgin olive oil

juice of ½ lemon

2 tablespoons pumpkin seeds, chopped

salt and pepper

FOR THE CONFIT GARLIC CLOVES

1 garlic bulb, cloves separated and peeled

olive oil

1   For the confit garlic, place the garlic cloves in a small saucepan and cover with olive oil. Cook over a very low heat for about 30 minutes or until the cloves are soft. Leave to cool, then transfer the cloves and oil to an airtight sterilized jar (see page 17) and keep in the refrigerator for up to 2–3 weeks.

2   Preheat the oven to 180°C fan, Gas Mark 6.

3   Place the butternut squash on a baking tray, drizzle with a little olive oil and season with salt and pepper. Roast for about 30 minutes until tender, then leave to cool.

4   Meanwhile, bring the water to the boil in a saucepan. Add the thyme and saffron, if using, take off the heat and leave to cool and infuse.

5   Blitz the chickpeas in a blender. Add all the remaining ingredients with the cooled squash and thyme and saffron infusion and blitz until smooth.

6   Correct the seasoning with salt and pepper to taste and keep chilled until ready to serve.

My first venture to Italy was in 1999 and I can still remember the moment when I tasted burrata – it was love at first bite! I don't get to Italy as much as I'd like to, but you will always find some burrata in my fridge at home. Served with a fennel salad and roast figs that bring it all together, I enjoy this combination of flavours so much that I even put it on the menu at the restaurant.

BURRATA, FENNEL & ROAST FIGS

SERVES 4

8 ripe figs

2 teaspoons honey

extra virgin olive oil

2 large fennel bulbs

juice of 1 lemon

¼ teaspoon fennel seeds, crushed

400g burrata

smoked paprika

salt and pepper

1 Preheat the oven to 190°C fan, Gas Mark 6½.

2 Cut a deep cross in the top of each fig and then gently squeeze the base to open it up like a flower. Place on a baking tray and drizzle with the honey and a little extra virgin olive oil. Roast for about 20 minutes until lightly golden.

3 Very thinly slice the fennel and place in a bowl of iced water until needed.

4 Make a dressing by mixing the lemon juice with 2 tablespoons of the extra virgin olive oil and the fennel seeds. Drain the sliced fennel, then lightly toss in the dressing.

5 Serve the burrata drizzled with a little olive oil and dusted with smoked paprika, alongside the roasted figs and fennel salad.

Mango season, when the fruit is at its juiciest, is a fantastic time of year, but this recipe uses green (in other words, not quite ripe) mangoes that are still firm, for a flavour that's slightly more sharp than sweet. Green mangoes really lend themselves to savoury dishes, taking on flavour and spice, and when you season them with salt, it opens up the flavours even more. This is an amazing dish.

CASHEW, CORIANDER & MANGO SALAD

SERVES 4–6

2 green (unripe) mangoes, peeled and pitted

1 small Hispi cabbage, finely shredded

1 small red onion, finely sliced

1 carrot, finely sliced or grated

1 red chilli, deseeded and finely sliced

50g cashew nuts, toasted

handful of coriander, roughly chopped

FOR THE DRESSING

grated zest and juice of 2 unwaxed limes

grated zest and juice of 1 unwaxed orange

2cm piece of fresh root ginger, peeled and grated

1 lemon grass stalk, tough outer leaves removed and tender stem finely chopped

20g dark muscovado sugar

50ml water

salt and pepper

1   Slice the mangoes thinly, then cut into strips. Place in a large bowl with the cabbage, onion, carrot and chilli.

2   For the dressing, whisk all the ingredients together and season to taste with salt and pepper.

3   Gently toss the salad in the dressing. Scatter the cashews and coriander on top and serve.

This is a great way to knock out a quick take on pizza –
especially when there's a group of young teens around waiting
to be fed during the summer holidays! Having some ready-made
tomato sauce on hand will make it even quicker. For alternative
filings, try stuffing these with pesto and chicken.

TOMATO & MUSHROOM PIZZA ROLLS

SERVES 4

250g button mushrooms, quartered
olive oil
1 batch of Pizza Dough (see pages 132–4)
1 batch of Tomato Sauce (see pages 132–4)
6 Italian tomatoes, thickly sliced
100g mild Cheddar cheese, grated
salt and pepper

1 Preheat the oven to 180°C fan, Gas Mark 6.

2 Cook the mushrooms in a little olive oil in a frying pan, then season
with a little salt and pepper.

3 Press the pizza dough out into a large flat rectangle, about 1cm thick.

4 Spread over the tomato sauce and top with the sliced tomato and mushrooms.
Sprinkle over the Cheddar, then roll up like a Swiss roll.

5 Cut into slices about 3cm thick and place in a deep baking tray, leaving
a 2cm gap between each slice. Cover and leave to prove at room
temperature for 20 minutes.

6 Meanwhile, increase the oven temperature to 190°C fan, Gas Mark 6½.

7 Bake the rolls for about 20 minutes until golden.

Plaice is a lovely fish that is easy to cook and serve whole because it doesn't have fish bones through it, but any flat fish works well here. This is reminiscent of our family seaside holidays together when the fishing boats have landed and you can buy your fish then and there – always the best way to buy fish. I like to serve this dish with a tomato salad and some steamed new potatoes.

BARBECUED PLAICE WITH ANCHOVY BUTTER & GRAPES

SERVES 4

olive oil

1kg whole plaice, scaled and gutted

2 fennel bulbs, finely sliced

2 preserved lemons, chopped

½ lemon, for squeezing

1 bunch of unseeded grapes

sea salt flakes and pepper

FOR THE ANCHOVY BUTTER

5 anchovy fillets, finely chopped

150g soft unsalted butter

1 garlic clove, grated

handful of flat leaf parsley, roughly chopped

1   For the anchovy butter, beat the anchovies through the soft butter with the garlic and parsley in a bowl. Keep chilled until needed.

2   Preheat a barbecue. Alternatively, preheat a large baking tray in the oven at 200°C fan, Gas Mark 7.

3   If using a barbecue, tear a large piece of foil big enough to wrap the fish in (omit this if oven cooking). Drizzle olive oil over the foil, or the preheated baking tray if using.

4   Season the fish with sea salt flakes and pepper and place on the foil or tray. Scatter the fennel and preserved lemons over the fish, then add a squeeze of lemon juice.

5   Bring the edges of the foil (if using) together over the fish and twist to seal, then repeat with the sides. Place the package – with the twisted seam facing down – on the hot barbecue and cook for 7 minutes. Carefully turn the package over and cook for a further 7 minutes. Alternatively, bake the fish in the oven for 10 minutes.

6   Place on a platter and leave to rest covered in foil for 3 minutes before serving.

7   Meanwhile, heat a small frying pan and cook the anchovy butter until foaming, being careful not to burn the butter. Add the grapes and quickly toss through the butter.

8   Uncover the fish and pop the butter and grapes on to the steaming fish. Serve immediately.

This salad is great on its own or as a side dish. We find it goes
so well with flatbreads and freshly made pesto that all you need
to add is a little sunshine and a glass of cold rosé! It's also lovely
served with my Manuka & Ras El Hanout Roast Lamb (see page 174),
if you're planning a bigger feast.

SPICY AUBERGINE & FETA WITH OVEN-DRIED TOMATOES

SERVES 4–6

2 tablespoons raisins

2 tablespoons white wine vinegar

40ml olive oil

2 large aubergines, cut into large cubes

2 courgettes, cut into large cubes

1–2 teaspoons chilli powder

1 tablespoon tomato purée

1 tablespoon honey

juice of ½ lemon

2 tablespoons chopped flat leaf parsley

1 small bunch of coriander, chopped

2 tablespoons pine nuts, toasted

100g feta cheese, crumbled

salt and pepper

FOR THE OVEN-DRIED TOMATOES

6 red cherry tomatoes, halved

6 yellow cherry tomatoes, halved

1 teaspoon thyme leaves

extra virgin olive oil

1   For the oven-dried tomatoes, preheat the oven to 120°C fan, Gas Mark 1.

2   Place the tomatoes on a baking tray, then season with salt and pepper, sprinkle with the thyme leaves and drizzle with extra virgin olive oil. Roast for 1 hour, then set aside and leave to cool.

3   Meanwhile, soak the raisins in the vinegar for 20 minutes, then drain.

4   Heat a large frying pan with the olive oil. Add the aubergines and cook over a medium-high heat until browned.

5   Reduce the heat, add the courgettes and cook gently for 10 minutes. Season with salt and the chilli powder to taste, then drain in a colander to remove any excess oil.

6   Return the aubergine and courgettes to the pan and stir in the tomato purée, honey and lemon juice, then take off the heat and leave to cool.

7   Gently mix in the herbs, pine nuts and tomatoes, then scatter with the feta and serve.

Our summer holiday meals are mainly based around the barbecue, no matter where we are in the world, and no matter what the weather is like! We also love a veggie burger option, especially one that's as delicious as this. Once the patties are made, they can be kept in the fridge until ready to cook.

SWEETCORN BURGER & ROCKET PESTO

MAKES 4

2 fresh corn on the cob

rapeseed oil

1 small onion, thinly sliced

1 garlic clove, thinly sliced

40g button mushrooms, quartered

1 teaspoon thyme leaves

400g can flageolet or haricot beans, drained

4 portobello mushrooms

salt and pepper

FOR THE ROCKET PESTO

1 garlic clove, peeled

2 bunches of rocket, about 100g in total

extra virgin olive oil

2 tablespoons pine nuts, lightly toasted

20g Parmesan cheese

½ lemon, for squeezing

FOR THE SPICED FLOUR

100g plain flour

¼ teaspoon crushed cumin seeds

¼ teaspoon crushed coriander seeds

¼ teaspoon smoked paprika

TO SERVE

4 burger buns

¼ small Iceberg lettuce, shredded

1 ripe beef tomato, sliced

100g soured cream

1 For the rocket pesto, pound the garlic to a paste with a pestle and mortar. Add the rocket in stages with a little extra virgin olive oil and the pine nuts, pounding after each addition. Grate in the Parmesan, stir through and season to taste with salt and pepper and a squeeze of lemon juice. Set aside.

2 Slice the corn kernels off the cobs.

3 Heat a frying pan over a medium heat and add a little oil. Add the onion and garlic and cook for 2 minutes, then add the button mushrooms and cook until lightly browned.

4 Stir in the thyme and corn, then take off the heat and leave to cool.

5 Mash the beans with a fork in a bowl, then mix in the cooled corn mixture and add a pinch of salt and pepper.

6 Divide the mixture into 4 equal amounts and press to form into nice thick patties.

7 For the spiced flour, mix all the ingredients together with some salt and pepper in a bowl.

8 Coat the patties with the spiced flour.

9 Preheat a barbecue, or griddle pan over a medium heat.

10 Brush the barbecue or griddle pan with oil and cook the patties for about 5–6 minutes until a nice golden colour, turning gently now and then. Remove and keep warm.

11 Add the portobellos and cook for about 2 minutes on each side, then season with salt and pepper.

12 Grill your buns.

13 Assemble the burgers in the buns with the lettuce, tomato, portobello mushrooms, a dollop of soured cream and the rocket pesto.

Sometimes, after many days of overindulging on holidays, it's a real treat to wind things back a bit and have something light and fresh such as this simple oregano chicken. The salad is of course optional, as is a glass of wine.

GRILLED CHICKEN WITH OREGANO & LEMON

SERVES 4

4 skinless chicken breasts
extra virgin olive oil
2 garlic cloves, grated
1 tablespoon oregano leaves
½ teaspoon thyme leaves
grated zest and juice of 1 unwaxed lemon (reserve the juice for the rocket salad)
salt and pepper

FOR THE ROCKET SALAD

1 tablespoon honey
1 tablespoon wholegrain mustard
juice of the zested lemon (see above)
100ml extra virgin olive oil
100g rocket
4 tarragon sprigs
handful of flat leaf parsley leaves

1 Place each chicken breast in a plastic bag or between 2 sheets of clingfilm and beat with a mallet or rolling pin to flatten until about 1cm thick.

2 Place the flattened chicken on a tray and drizzle with extra virgin olive oil. Add the garlic, herbs, lemon zest and salt and pepper, then rub into the chicken all over. Cover and leave to marinate in the refrigerator for 1–2 hours.

3 For the rocket salad, whisk the honey, mustard, lemon juice and extra virgin olive oil together in a bowl and season with salt and pepper. Gently toss the rocket and herbs through the dressing.

4 Preheat a griddle pan over a high heat or a barbecue.

5 Sear the chicken for 2 minutes on each side or until cooked through, then serve with the rocket salad.

On one of my visits to Morocco, I was fortunate enough to be able to make my own ras el hanout spice blend. And any time a friend is visiting that country, I ask them to bring a bag back. Rubbed into lamb and roasted with a little honey, this has got to be one of the best ways to enjoy it. If you don't have manuka honey, any type of honey will do just fine.

MANUKA & RAS EL HANOUT ROAST LAMB

SERVES 4-6

2kg leg of lamb

1 tablespoon sea salt flakes

3 tablespoons manuka honey

2 tablespoons ras el hanout

1 tablespoon hot water

5 rosemary sprigs

1   Preheat the oven to 140°C fan, Gas Mark 3.

2   Trim the lamb of any excess fat. Using a sharp knife, score the surface of the lamb at intervals all over, then pierce throughout with the tip of the knife. Rub the lamb all over with the sea salt.

3   Mix the honey and spice with the hot water and rub or brush all over the lamb.

4   Break up the rosemary into smaller sprigs and poke into the incisions.

5   Place the lamb in a large roasting tray, then cover with foil and roast for 1 hour. Baste and turn the lamb over, then cover again and roast for a further 45 minutes.

6   Remove the foil and baste again, then roast uncovered for a final 15 minutes.

7   Baste once more, then turn off the oven and leave the lamb inside for 20 minutes with the door ajar before serving. This allows the meat to rest and stay warm at the same time while you enjoy an aperitif – or two!

Many moons ago I made a wonderful friend, Rose. She comes from China (where we met) and has recently celebrated her 80th birthday! She introduced me to cooking with cola, and since then I've adapted my ribs recipe to include it. This version is a hit with friends and family, and they are always thrilled to hear about the addition of cola. Spare ribs can go straight into the oven or on the barbecue, but simmering them in water for a few minutes first helps break down the protein that can otherwise take a long time to cook down, making the ribs even more tender. These are great served with coleslaw and flatbreads.

COLA & SPICE-GLAZED PORK SPARE RIBS

SERVES 4

2kg pork spare ribs

handful of sea salt flakes

3 bay leaves

6 star anise

2 cinnamon sticks

FOR THE MARINADE

330ml can cola

300g tomato ketchup

80g hoisin sauce

2 garlic cloves, grated

2 tablespoons Worcestershire sauce

2 teaspoons chilli powder

1 teaspoon smoked paprika

½ teaspoon sea salt flakes

1   Place the ribs in a large saucepan. Add the sea salt flakes, bay leaves and the spices and cover with cold water.

2   Bring to the boil and skim the surface, then reduce the heat and simmer for 15 minutes.

3   Take off the heat and leave the ribs to rest in the cooking liquid for 10 minutes, then drain.

4   Meanwhile, preheat the oven to 190°C fan, Gas Mark 6½, or heat a barbecue.

5   Mix all the marinade ingredients together in a bowl. Rub or brush into the ribs, reserving any excess marinade. Place the ribs in a large roasting tray and cook for 12 minutes.

6   Turn the ribs over and pour over the remaining marinade to cover, then return to the oven for a further 12 minutes. To serve, carefully cut between the ribs to separate.

It's no secret that I adore dark chocolate, so this tart is right up there for me as a chocolate fix. With the addition of the spices, it makes for a great dessert during the Christmas season. I like to use poached pears here, but if you want to use canned fruit, that's fine too. And if you omit the spices, the recipe will also work beautifully with soft fruits.

DARK CHOCOLATE & PEAR TART

SERVES 10

450ml red wine
100g caster sugar
3 small Conference pears

FOR THE BISCUIT BASE

200g packet digestive biscuits
2 pinches of ground cinnamon
pinch of ground nutmeg
pinch of ground ginger
100g unsalted butter, melted

FOR THE GANACHE

350g dark chocolate (70% cocoa)
300ml whipping cream
20g glucose syrup
100g unsalted butter, melted

1 Line the base and sides of a 20cm diameter cake tin with nonstick baking paper.

2 For the biscuit base, place the digestives in a food processor with the spices and pulse to a crumb, then stir in the melted butter. Press into the base of the prepared tin. Keep chilled until needed.

3 Place the wine and sugar in a saucepan just big enough to fit the pears, and bring to the boil.

4 Meanwhile, peel the pears. Add them to the pan and make sure they are covered by the wine. Reduce the heat to low and simmer gently for 10–15 minutes or until the pears are nice and tender – test by inserting a cocktail stick. Leave to cool completely in the poaching liquid. Lift the pears out, then cut into quarters, remove the core and drain on kitchen paper.

5 For the ganache, break the chocolate into small pieces and place in a heatproof bowl.

6 Bring the cream and glucose to the boil in a small saucepan. Pour the cream mixture over the chocolate while stirring continuously. Stir in the butter until everything has combined.

7 Pour the ganache on to the biscuit base, then gently push in the poached pears. Leave to set in refrigerator for at least 1½ hours or overnight.

This is very similar to a millefeuille with all the layers.
My twist on the traditional dessert is to use the classic flavour
combination of coffee and walnuts, which not surprisingly
works so well with the puff pastry and rich whipped cream.

WALNUT & COFFEE PASTRY LAYER CAKE

SERVES 6–8

200ml water

200g caster sugar

1 x 320g sheet of ready-rolled puff pastry

plain flour, for dusting

100g unsalted butter

140g walnuts, roughly chopped and toasted

200g dark chocolate (70% cocoa), shaved

1 tablespoon icing sugar

FOR THE COFFEE CREAM

400ml milk

1 teaspoon vanilla bean paste or seeds scraped from 1 vanilla pod

15g espresso instant coffee powder

8 egg yolks (140g in total)

100g caster sugar

40g cornflour

20g plain flour

160g cold unsalted butter, cubed

160g soft unsalted butter

1 Bring the water and sugar to the boil in a saucepan and boil for 1 minute, then leave to cool.

2 Roll out the pastry on a lightly floured work surface as thinly as possible – about 1mm. Cut out large circles about 20cm in diameter – you should get 6–7 out of the sheet. Prick all over with a fork.

3 Heat a little of the butter in a wide frying pan and gently fry each pastry circle on both sides until golden and crispy, then set them aside to cool.

4 For the coffee cream, heat the milk with the vanilla and coffee in a saucepan.

5 Meanwhile whisk the egg yolks, sugar and flours together in a bowl. Pour over the hot milk mixture while whisking continuously. Return the mixture to the pan and cook over a medium-low heat, whisking continuously, until very thick.

6 Take off the heat and, while hot, gradually whisk in the cold butter cubes. Leave to cool, then whisk in the soft butter.

7 To assemble, dip each crispy puff pastry circle into the syrup and sandwich together with a layer of the coffee cream in between.

8 Pipe the remaining coffee cream on top to decorate, and sprinkle with the toasted walnuts and dark chocolate shavings. Dust gently with the icing sugar. Slice the cake into portions to serve.

Okay, okay, so I made a dessert based on my favourite cocktail –
need I say more? We've all heard about lime cheesecake, but add
tequila and Cointreau and then you're talking my language.

MARGARITA (TEQUILA, COINTREAU & LIME) CHEESECAKE

SERVES 6

100g muscovado sugar

grated zest and juice of 4 unwaxed limes

2 tablespoons tequila

1 teaspoon vanilla bean paste or seeds
scraped from 1 vanilla pod

600g cream cheese

100g single cream

FOR THE BISCUIT BASE

150g digestive biscuits

50g rolled oats, toasted

100g salted butter, melted

2 tablespoons Cointreau

1   For the biscuit base, place all the ingredients in a food processor and pulse to a crumb. Press into a 20cm springform cake tin and halfway up the sides, then chill to set.

2   Mix the sugar, lime juice, tequila and vanilla together in a large bowl, then add the remaining ingredients and whisk together until you have a light mixture.

3   Pour into the biscuit base, then refrigerate for a minimum of 2 hours or overnight to set before serving.

It seems wrong not to include this recipe here. Hot cross buns were always a must in our home while growing up. I still prefer them the way Mum would serve them – toasted with lots of butter melting through them. I think the first time I made hot cross buns was for my little brother to take into school for Easter, which is going back some years, as he's now well into his thirties!

HOT CROSS BUNS

MAKES 12

300ml milk

50g unsalted butter

8g fresh yeast

1 teaspoon caster sugar, plus an extra 2 tablespoons

100g strong wholemeal flour, plus extra for dusting

400g strong white flour

1 teaspoon ground cinnamon

½ teaspoon mixed spice

½ teaspoon ground nutmeg

100g currants

100g raisins

80g mixed candied peel, chopped

1 large egg

rapeseed oil

80g warm manuka honey

FOR THE CROSS

70g plain flour

80ml water

1 Warm the milk with the butter in a saucepan. Crumble in the yeast and whisk in with 1 teaspoon of the sugar.

2 Mix together the flours, spices, dried fruit, candied peel and the remaining 2 tablespoons of sugar in a large bowl. Make a well in the centre, add the egg, pour in the yeast mixture and gradually mix in to form a dough.

3 Turn the dough out on a lightly floured work surface and knead for about 10 minutes until smooth and elastic. Lightly oil a clean bowl, then add the dough, cover and leave in a warm place for about an hour or until doubled in size.

4 Push the dough down in the centre and knead lightly. Divide into 12 equal-sized pieces and shape into balls. Place on a large, oiled baking tray about 2cm apart, cover and leave in a warm place for about an hour or until doubled in size.

5 Meanwhile, preheat the oven to 190°C fan, Gas Mark 6½.

6 For the paste, mix the flour and the water together, then place in a small piping bag. Pipe a cross on top of each bun, then bake for 20–25 minutes until golden.

7 Transfer to a wire rack and brush with the warm honey to glaze.

I first made this variation on an old favourite using leftover stale hot cross buns. I hate to throw anything away, so they found their way into a bread and butter pudding. If you only have a few hot cross buns like I did, you can make up the difference with normal bread with the crusts removed, or it works just as well with croissants. And here's a tip if you have any leftover Christmas pudding: sprinkle chunks of that across the top when you add the currants.

HOT CROSS BUN BREAD & BUTTER PUDDING

SERVES 4–6

150g soft unsalted butter

12 hot cross buns (see page 181 for homemade)

handful of currants

400ml double cream

300ml milk

120g caster sugar, plus extra for the topping

12 egg yolks

1 teaspoon vanilla bean paste or seeds scraped from 2 vanilla pods

1   Preheat the oven to 160°C fan, Gas Mark 4.

2   Take a baking dish about 32 x 23cm and grease with some of the butter.

3   Cut the buns in half and butter the cut sides. Arrange the bun halves in the baking dish, buttered side up, in rows, sprinkling the currants in between.

4   Bring the cream and milk to the boil in a saucepan.

5   Meanwhile, whisk the sugar, egg yolks and vanilla bean paste or seeds together in a bowl until just mixed.

6   Pour the hot cream mixture over the sugar and egg yolks while whisking continuously. Return the mixture to the pan and cook over a medium-low heat, stirring continuously, until thick enough to coat the back of a wooden spoon – just before the custard comes to the boil, or when it reaches 82°C on a sugar thermometer.

7   Pour the custard over the buns and leave to sit for 10 minutes.

8   Bake for 25–30 minutes until set. Remove from the oven and turn the oven to the grill function.

9   Sprinkle the top liberally with sugar and place under the hot grill to caramelize.

I came up with these a few years ago for Christmas and they make a great treat at the end of the meal – and a great alternative to a steamed Christmas pudding. Triple the recipe and stack them high...

CHOCOLATE BRANDY SNAPS WITH ORANGE MARMALADE CHANTILLY

MAKES 20–22

120g caster sugar

60g soft unsalted butter

60g golden syrup

20g plain flour

1 teaspoon cocoa powder

pinch of ground nutmeg

pinch of ground cloves

FOR THE ORANGE MARMALADE CHANTILLY

300ml double cream

100g soured cream

1 tablespoon icing sugar

seeds scraped from 1 vanilla pod

70g orange marmalade

1 For the orange marmalade chantilly, whip the double cream and soured cream with the icing sugar and vanilla seeds in a bowl to stiff peaks. Gently fold through the marmalade, then chill.

2 Preheat the oven to 150°C fan, Gas Mark 3½.

3 Whisk the sugar, butter and golden syrup together in a bowl.

4 Sift the flour, cocoa powder and spices together, then whisk into the golden syrup mixture to form a paste.

5 Working in batches, spread the paste into large circles, about 8cm in diameter and 1.5mm thick, on to a large nonstick baking mat. Place the mat on a large baking tray and bake for 15–20 minutes until bubbling and dark chocolate in colour.

6 Remove from the oven and leave to sit for 4–5 minutes. While still quite warm, quickly roll the circles around the thick handle of a wooden spoon or balloon whisk, about 3cm in diameter, then slide off and leave to cool and harden on a wire rack.

7 Pipe the chantilly into either end of the brandy snaps before serving.

I never truly appreciated these treats until I was left to make hundreds of them when I first moved to the UK more than 20 years ago! After trying many, many different types, I make mine with the addition of pistachios and chestnuts. I find the mincemeat really develops when you prepare it a few days ahead so that all the spices and juices have macerated together. I put a star shape on mine only because it's how my daughter prefers them – a family tradition.

MY MINCE PIES

MAKES 12

120g soft unsalted butter

60g caster sugar

1 small egg, plus 1 egg, beaten, for glazing

180g plain flour, plus extra for dusting

1 tablespoon water

icing sugar, for dusting

FOR THE MINCEMEAT (MAKES ABOUT 1KG)

200g Bramley apple, peeled, cored and grated

120g raisins

120g currants

100g candied orange peel, chopped

80g cooked chestnuts, chopped

60g pistachio nuts, chopped

50g soft light brown sugar

25g suet

grated zest and juice of 1 unwaxed orange

grated zest and juice of 1 unwaxed lemon

¼ teaspoon ground nutmeg

¼ teaspoon ground cloves

¼ teaspoon ground cinnamon

100ml brandy

1   Prepare the mincemeat a few days ahead: Mix all the ingredients together in a large bowl, spoon into airtight sterilized jars (see page 17), and store in the refrigerator to allow the flavours to develop. Use within 2–3 weeks.

2   For the pastry, beat the butter and sugar together in a bowl until fully creamed, then beat in the egg. Fold in the flour without overmixing.

3   Add the water as needed to bring the mixture together into a dough. Wrap and chill for 30 minutes.

4   Preheat the oven to 180°C fan, Gas Mark 6.

5   Roll out the pastry on a lightly floured work surface to about 3mm thick. Using a round cutter (about 9cm), cut out circles large enough to line 12 holes of a muffin tin.

6   Spoon the mincemeat into the lined moulds until three-quarters filled.

7   Using a star cutter, cut out 10 stars for lids, cover the pies and press on to the pastry edges to seal. Brush the tops with the beaten egg to glaze.

8   Bake for 20–25 minutes until lightly golden. Cool on a wire rack. Serve warm, dusted with a little icing sugar.

This recipe is my take on traditional Samoan coconut buns that
my family has always made and enjoyed over Christmas. These soft,
sweet buns are best served straight from the baking tin to share.

COCONUT & FRUIT MINCEMEAT BUNS

MAKES 12

250g strong white flour, plus extra for dusting

pinch of salt

150ml milk

25g caster sugar

5g fresh yeast

150g Quick Mincemeat (see below)

25g desiccated coconut, toasted

50g soft unsalted butter, plus extra for the top

50g demerara sugar

400ml coconut milk (shake the can before opening)

FOR THE QUICK MINCEMEAT (MAKES ABOUT 350G)

100g Bramley apple, peeled, cored and grated

75g raisins

75g currants

50g candied orange peel, chopped

grated zest and juice of 1 unwaxed orange

grated zest and juice of 1 unwaxed lemon

30g light brown soft sugar

50g frozen lard, grated

¼ teaspoon each of ground nutmeg, cinnamon and cloves

1 tablespoon brandy

1 For the mincemeat, mix all the ingredients together in a bowl, spoon into sterilized airtight jars (see page 17), and store in the refrigerator for up to 2–3 weeks.

2 Mix the flour and salt together in a large bowl and make a well in the centre.

3 Heat the milk with the caster sugar in a saucepan until warm. Crumble in the yeast and stir in. Pour the yeast mixture into the flour and gradually mix in to form a dough.

4 Knead the dough on a lightly floured work surface for about 4 minutes until smooth and elastic. Return to the bowl, cover and leave in a warm place for an hour or until doubled in size.

5 Knock back the dough and knead lightly, then roll out into a large rectangle about 1cm thick.

6 Spread the mincemeat over the dough and sprinkle over the toasted coconut. Roll up the dough like a Swiss roll and cut into slices about 4cm thick.

7 Take a shallow baking tin about 30 x 25cm and spread the butter over the base. Sprinkle over the demerara sugar, reserving 10g, then pour over the coconut milk.

8 Place the bun slices in the coconut milk, leaving 1cm gaps in between. Cover and leave to prove in a warm place for 40 minutes or until well risen and the gaps have been filled by the proved dough.

9 Meanwhile, preheat the oven to 180°C fan, Gas Mark 6.

10 Place a small knob of extra butter on top of each bun and sprinkle with the reserved demerara sugar. Bake for 25–30 minutes or until golden brown. Gently separate the buns using a spoon before serving

INDEX

AUTHOR'S ACKNOWLEDGEMENTS

Thanks to the Octopus team for making it so easy to get the project together.

The amazing Yuki for capturing my food in such a special way.

Thanks to Karen Taylor and Alicia Boardman for the brilliant food sourcing, prep and edits during the shoots.

Thanks to Churchill for the beautiful selection of plates, and Picualia for the best olive oil!

My lovely agent Rosemary for always having my back!

To all of you who've supported and broken bread with me over the years, here's to many more happy memories together...

ABOUT THE AUTHOR

Born in Samoa and brought up in New Zealand, chef Monica Galetti moved to the UK in 1999. Monica worked alongside chef Michel Roux Jr at London's acclaimed Le Gavroche, and became a household name in 2008 when she joined the BBC2 team as a judge on *Masterchef – The Professionals*. She has gone on to co-present BBC2's *Amazing Hotels – Life Beyond the Lobby*.

She opened her own restaurant in 2017 – the award-winning Mere – alongside her husband David Galetti. Her home life revolves around her daughter Anais and dogs Fynn (a boxer) and Cole (a Frenchie).

 @galettigram

 @MGaletti01